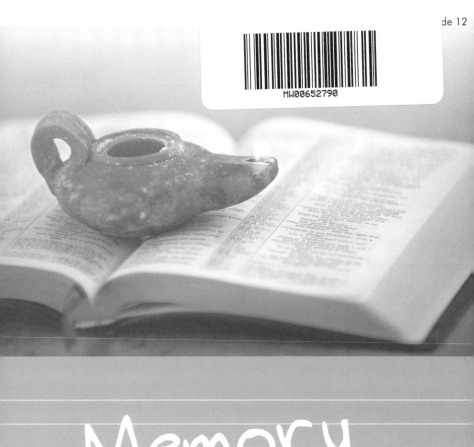

Memory Work
NOTEBOOK

Compiled by

PAUL G. SETTLE

PUBLICATION HISTORY

Memory Work Notebook was first published in 1962 by the Christian Education Committee of Trinity Presbyterian Church in Montgomery, Alabama. The author, Rev. Paul G. Settle, was associate pastor of the church at the time. Later editions were released in 1967, 1970 and 1974.

Great Commission Publications began publishing the volume in 1989, incorporating the Scripture memory verses in two translations—NIV and NKJV. This 2005 revision introduced the ESV alongside the NKJV.

Two catechisms are included in age-appropriate increments: *First Catechism* (GCP's revision of the original Catechism for Young Children) for ages four to nine, and the *Westminster Shorter Catechism* for ages 10 and older.

5th Printing 2015

Scripture quotations are from two versions of the Bible: The New King James Version, copyright © 1979, 1980, 1982, Thomas Nelson Inc., publishers; and The ESV® Bible (The Holy Bible, English Standard Version®), copyright © 2001 by Crossway. Used by permission. All rights reserved.

ISBN 0-934688-55-9

Published by Great Commission Publications
3640 Windsor Park Drive
Suwanee, GA 30024-3897

INTRODUCTION

You are a young person with the opportunity to know God even better. Or you may be a Christian parent or teacher—perhaps both. In any case remember how vitally important it is for the disciples of Jesus Christ to hide God's Word in their hearts. It is also very meaningful to understand the structure of systematic truth in the Bible. When you see the whole, you understand the parts better.

To help you do both is the purpose of this Notebook. Important Bible verses are listed for age 3 through grade 12. Catechism questions and answers are also included to help you summarize what the Bible says about God, about us and about the world in which we live. Also note that various hymns are suggested for each age group. For when you learn about our gracious God, you will want to praise him.

First Catechism—a revision (2003) based on the Catechism for Young Children—is used for children from age 3 through grade 4. This is a simplified teaching tool to help younger children learn the basics of our faith and doctrine. The Shorter Catechism then is used for children in grade 5 and older. It is part of the Westminster Standards, written in the 17th century, which serve as the doctrinal foundation of Presbyterian churches worldwide.

With all of these resources printed in the book, young people have easy access to them. Parents can readily help everyone in the household memorize during family worship or at other times. Many churches use the Notebook to conduct a program whereby children memorize at home and recite passages to a teacher at church. The Bible memory selections correspond in part to texts covered in the GCP Sunday school curriculum.

The Bible verses have been printed in two reliable, modern translations, the New King James Version and the English Standard Version.

Now it's up to you. Memorize the Word of God and teach the great truths God has revealed.

Paul G. Settle

Publisher's Note

Further aids are available for teaching the materials found in *Memory Work Notebook:*

- *First Catechism.* Appropriate for ages 3 through 9.
- *Kids' Quest! Catechism Club.* Program to teach and memorize *First Catechism.*
- The Shorter Catechism. Available in several editions from Great Commission Publications.
- *How to Teach the Catechism to Children* by Joyce M. Horton. Includes comments on each question, teaching tips and guidelines for organizing a catechetical program.
- *The Shorter Catechism: A Study Manual* by G. I. Williamson. Can be used as a student text and teacher's guide.
- *Trinity Hymnal.* Contains most of the hymns used in this Notebook.
- *Why Can't I See God?* by Judy Rogers. Twenty songs on cassette tape based on the original Catechism for Young Children and the Shorter Catechism.
- Bible Doctrine. A study for junior highs based on the Shorter Catechism. Includes the student paper Focus. Divided into two "years" of 30 lessons each.
- *Q&A.* Fliers/bulletin inserts to help you teach the Shorter Catechism to your congregation.

For further information on these and other catechetical resources contact Great Commission Publications, 3640 Windsor Park Drive, Suwanee, GA 30024-3897. Phone: 800-695-3387. Website: www.gcp.org.

MEMORY WORK

Age 3

Genesis 1:1

In the beginning God created the heavens and the earth. *NKJV*

In the beginning, God created the heavens and the earth. *ESV*

Date _____ Parent/Teacher _____

Matthew 22:37

Jesus said to him, "You shall love the Lord your God with all your heart, with all your soul, and with all your mind." *NKJV*

And he said to him, "You shall love the Lord your God with all your heart and with all your soul and with all your mind." *ESV*

Date _____ Parent/Teacher _____

John 3:16

For God so loved the world that He gave His only begotten Son, that whoever believes in Him should not perish but have everlasting life. *NKJV*

For God so loved the world, that he gave his only Son, that whoever believes in him should not perish but have eternal life. *ESV*

Date _____ Parent/Teacher _____

Matthew 22:39

You shall love your neighbor as yourself. *NKJV*

You shall love your neighbor as yourself. *ESV*

Date _____ Parent/Teacher _____

Luke 19:10

For the Son of Man has come
to seek and to save that which
was lost. *NKJV*

For the Son of Man came to
seek and to save the lost.
ESV

Date _____ Parent/Teacher _____

John 10:11

I am the good shepherd. The
good shepherd gives His life
for the sheep. *NKJV*

I am the good shepherd. The
good shepherd lays down his
life for the sheep. *ESV*

Date _____ Parent/Teacher _____

Song of Songs 2:4

He brought me to the banquet-
ing house, and his banner over
me was love. *NKJV*

He brought me to the banquet-
ing house, and his banner over
me was love. *ESV*

Date _____ Parent/Teacher _____

Colossians 4:2

Continue earnestly in prayer, being vigilant in it with thanksgiving. *NKJV*

Continue steadfastly in prayer, being watchful in it with thanksgiving. *ESV*

Date _____ Parent/Teacher _____

First Catechism

1. *Q. Who made you?*
   A. God.

2. *Q. What else did God make?*
   A. God made all things.

3. *Q. Why did God make you and all things?*
   A. For his own glory.

4. *Q. How can you glorify God?*
   A. By loving him and doing what he commands.

5. *Q. Why are you to glorify God?*
   A. Because he made me and takes care of me.

Date _____ Parent/Teacher _____

Songs

"Jesus Loves Me" (stanzas 1, 2)

Date _____ Parent/Teacher _____

Age 3

"A Little Child May Know"

Date _____ Parent/Teacher _____

Supplemental Notes

MEMORY WORK

Age 4

Acts 16:31

Believe on the Lord Jesus Christ, and you will be saved, you and your household. *NKJV*

Believe in the Lord Jesus, and you will be saved, you and your household. *ESV*

Date _____ Parent/Teacher _____

Mark 10:14

Let the little children come to Me, and do not forbid them; for of such is the kingdom of God. *NKJV*

Let the children come to me; do not hinder them, for to such belongs the kingdom of God. *ESV*

Date _____ Parent/Teacher _____

Ephesians 6:2

Honor your father and mother. *NKJV*

Honor your father and mother. *ESV*

Date _____ Parent/Teacher _____

Psalm 23:1

The LORD is my shepherd; I shall not want. *NKJV*

The LORD is my shepherd; I shall not want. *ESV*

Date _____ Parent/Teacher _____

Psalm 122:1

I was glad when they said to me, "Let us go into the house of the LORD." *NKJV*

I was glad when they said to me, "Let us go to the house of the LORD!" *ESV*

Date _____ Parent/Teacher _____

John 4:24

God is Spirit, and those who worship Him must worship in spirit and truth. *NKJV*

God is spirit, and those who worship him must worship in spirit and truth. *ESV*

Date _____ Parent/Teacher _____

Matthew 11:28

Come to Me, all you who labor and are heavy laden, and I will give you rest. *NKJV*

Come to me, all who labor and are heavy laden, and I will give you rest. *ESV*

Date _____ Parent/Teacher _____

John 8:12

Then Jesus spoke to them again, saying, "I am the light of the world. He who follows Me shall not walk in darkness, but have the light of life." *NKJV*

Again Jesus spoke to them, saying, "I am the light of the world. Whoever follows me will not walk in darkness, but will have the light of life." *ESV*

Date _____ Parent/Teacher _____

First Catechism

6. *Q. Is there more than one true God?*
   A. No. There is only one true God.

7. *Q. In how many Persons does this one God exist?*
   A. In three Persons.

8. *Q. Name these three Persons.*
   A. The Father, the Son and the Holy Spirit.

9. *Q. What is God?*
   A. God is a Spirit and does not have a body like men.

10. *Q. Where is God?*
    A. God is everywhere.

11. *Q. Can you see God?*
    A. No. I cannot see God, but he always sees me.

12. *Q. Does God know all things?*
    A. Yes. Nothing can be hidden from God.

13. *Q. Can God do all things?*
    A. Yes. God can do all his holy will.

14. *Q. Where do you learn how to love and obey God?*
    A. In the Bible alone.

15. *Q. Who wrote the Bible?*
    A. Chosen men who were inspired by the Holy Spirit.

Date _____ Parent/Teacher _____

The Lord's Prayer (Matthew 6:9–13)

[9]Our Father which art in heaven, hallowed be thy name.

[10]Thy kingdom come. Thy will be done on earth, as it is in heaven.

[11]Give us this day our daily bread.

[12]And forgive us our debts, as we forgive our debtors.

[13]And lead us not into temptation, but deliver us from evil. For thine is the kingdom, and the power, and the glory, for ever. Amen. *NKJV*

[9]Our Father in heaven, Hallowed be Your name.

[10]Your kingdom come. Your will be done on earth as it is in heaven.

[11]Give us this day our daily bread.

[12]And forgive us our debts, as we forgive our debtors.

[13]And do not lead us into temptation, but deliver us from the evil one. For Yours is the kingdom and the power and the glory forever. Amen. *NKJV*

[9]Our Father in heaven, hallowed be your name.

[10]Your kingdom come, your will be done, on earth as it is in heaven.

[11]Give us this day our daily bread,

[12]and forgive us our debts, as we also have forgiven our debtors.

[13]And lead us not into temptation, but deliver us from evil. *ESV*

Date _____ Parent/Teacher _____

Songs

"God, Who Made the Earth"

Date _____ Parent/Teacher _____

"Praise Him! Praise Him!"

Date _____ Parent/Teacher _____

"Can a Little Child like Me?"

Date _____ Parent/Teacher _____

"O Little Town of Bethlehem"

Date _____ Parent/Teacher _____

Supplemental Notes

MEMORY WORK

Age 5

Romans 6:23

For the wages of sin is death, but the gift of God is eternal life in Christ Jesus our Lord. *NKJV*

For the wages of sin is death, but the free gift of God is eternal life in Christ Jesus our Lord. *ESV*

Date _____ Parent/Teacher _____

John 6:35

And Jesus said to them, "I am the bread of life. He who comes to Me shall never hunger, and he who believes in Me shall never thirst." *NKJV*

Jesus said to them, "I am the bread of life; whoever comes to me shall not hunger, and whoever believes in me shall never thirst." *ESV*

Date _____ Parent/Teacher _____

John 10:9

I am the door. If anyone enters by Me, he will be saved, and will go in and out and find pasture. *NKJV*

I am the door. If anyone enters by me, he will be saved and will go in and out and find pasture. *ESV*

Date _____ Parent/Teacher _____

Psalm 23

¹The LORD is my shepherd; I shall not want.

²He makes me to lie down in green pastures; He leads me beside the still waters.

³He restores my soul; He leads me in the paths of righteousness for His name's sake.

⁴Yea, though I walk through the valley of the shadow of death, I will fear no evil; for You are with me; Your rod and Your staff, they comfort me.

⁵You prepare a table before me in the presence of my enemies; You anoint my head with oil; my cup runs over.

⁶Surely goodness and mercy shall follow me all the days of my life; and I will dwell in the house of the LORD forever.
NKJV

¹The LORD is my shepherd; I shall not want.

²He makes me lie down in green pastures. He leads me beside still waters.

³He restores my soul. He leads me in paths of righteousness for his name's sake.

⁴Even though I walk through the valley of the shadow of death, I will fear no evil, for you are with me; your rod and your staff, they comfort me.

⁵You prepare a table before me in the presence of my enemies; you anoint my head with oil; my cup overflows.

⁶Surely goodness and mercy shall follow me all the days of my life, and I shall dwell in the house of the LORD forever.
ESV

Date _____ Parent/Teacher _____

Deuteronomy 6:4, 5

⁴Hear, O Israel; The LORD our God, the LORD is one!

⁴Hear, O Israel: The LORD our God, the LORD is one.

⁵You shall love the LORD your God with all your heart, with all your soul, and with all your might. *NKJV*

⁵You shall love the LORD your God with all your heart and with all your soul and with all your might. *ESV*

Date _____ Parent/Teacher _____

John 1:29

The next day John saw Jesus coming toward him, and said, "Behold! The Lamb of God who takes away the sin of the world!" *NKJV*

The next day he saw Jesus coming toward him, and said, "Behold, the Lamb of God, who takes away the sin of the world!" *ESV*

Date _____ Parent/Teacher _____

Psalm 91:2

I will say of the LORD, "He is my refuge and my fortress; my God, in Him I will trust." *NKJ*

I will say to the LORD, "My refuge and my fortress, my God, in whom I trust." *ESV*

Date _____ Parent/Teacher _____

First Catechism

16. *Q. Who were our first parents?*
   A. Adam and Eve.

17. *Q. How did God create man?*
   A. God created man, male and female, after his own image.

18. *Q. Of what were our first parents made?*
   A. God made Adam's body out of the ground and Eve's body out of a rib from Adam.

19. Q. *What else did God give Adam and Eve* besides bodies?
    A. He gave them souls that will last forever.

20. Q. *Do you have a soul as well as a body?*
    A. Yes. And my soul is going to last forever.

21. Q. *How do you know your soul will last forever?*
    A. Because the Bible tells me so.

22. Q. *In what condition did God make Adam and Eve?*
    A. He made them holy and happy.

23. Q. *What covenant did God make with Adam?*
    A. The covenant of life.

24. Q. *What is a covenant?*
    A. A relationship that God establishes with us and guarantees by his word.

25. Q. *In the covenant of life, what did God require Adam to do?*
    A. To obey God perfectly.

26. Q. *What did God promise in the covenant of life?*
    A. To reward Adam with life if he obeyed God perfectly.

27. Q. *What did God threaten in the covenant of life?*
    A. To punish Adam with death if he disobeyed God.

28. Q. *Did Adam keep the covenant of life?*
    A. No. He sinned against God.

29. Q. *What is sin?*
    A. Sin is any lack of conformity to, or transgression of, the law of God.

30. Q. *What is meant by lack of conformity?*
    A. Not being or doing what God requires.

31. Q. *What is meant by transgression?*
   A. Doing what God forbids.

Date _____ Parent/Teacher _____

The Doxology

Praise God from whom all blessings flow. Praise him all creatures here below. Praise him above ye heavenly host. Praise Father, Son and Holy Ghost. Amen.

Date _____ Parent/Teacher _____

The Gloria Patri

Glory be to the Father, and to the Son and to the Holy Ghost. As it was in the beginning, is now and ever shall be, world without end. Amen. Amen.

Date _____ Parent/Teacher _____

Hymns

"Tell Me the Story of Jesus"

Date _____ Parent/Teacher _____

"Away in a Manger"

Date _____ Parent/Teacher _____

"Unto the Hills"

Date _____ Parent/Teacher _____

"The Lord's My Shepherd"

Date _____ Parent/Teacher _____

Supplemental Notes

MEMORY WORK

Grade 1

Names of the Twelve Apostles

These are the twelve apostles' names:
Peter, Andrew, John and James.
Two pairs of brothers who fished by the sea
When Jesus said to them, "Follow me."
James the Less, and Jude were called, too;
Philip, also Bartholomew.
Matthew, and Thomas who doubted his word;
Simon, and Judas who sold his Lord.

Date _____ Parent/Teacher _____

Luke 2:8-15

8Now there were in the same country shepherds living out in the fields, keeping watch over their flock by night.

9And behold, an angel of the Lord stood before them, and the glory of the Lord shone around them, and they were greatly afraid.

10Then the angel said to them, "Do not be afraid, for behold, I bring you good tidings of great joy which will be to all people.

8And in the same region there were shepherds out in the field, keeping watch over their flock by night.

9And an angel of the Lord appeared to them, and the glory of the Lord shone around them, and they were filled with fear.

10And the angel said to them, "Fear not, for behold, I bring you good news of a great joy that will be for all the people.

21

¹¹For there is born to you this day in the city of David a Savior, who is Christ the Lord.

¹²And this will be the sign to you: You will find a Babe wrapped in swaddling cloths, lying in a manger."

¹³And suddenly there was with the angel a multitude of the heavenly host praising God and saying:

¹⁴"Glory to God in the highest, and on earth peace, good will toward men!"

¹⁵So it was, when the angels had gone away from them into heaven, that the shepherds said to one another, "Let us now go to Bethlehem and see this thing that has come to pass, which the Lord has made known to us." *NKJV*

¹¹For unto you is born this day in the city of David a Savior, who is Christ the Lord.

¹²And this will be a sign for you: you will find a baby wrapped in swaddling cloths and lying in a manger."

¹³And suddenly there was with the angel a multitude of the heavenly host praising God and saying,

¹⁴"Glory to God in the highest, and on earth peace among those with whom he is pleased!"

¹⁵When the angels went away from them into heaven, the shepherds said to one another, "Let us go over to Bethlehem and see this thing that has happened, which the Lord has made known to us." *ESV*

Date _____ Parent/Teacher _____

John 11:25, 26

²⁵Jesus said to her, "I am the resurrection and the life. He who believes in Me, though he may die, he shall live.

²⁵Jesus said to her, "I am the resurrection and the life. Whoever believes in me, though he die, yet shall he live,

²⁶And whoever lives and believes in Me shall never die. Do you believe this?" *NKJV*

²⁶and everyone who lives and believes in me shall never die. Do you believe this?" *ESV*

Date _____ Parent/Teacher _____

Psalm 8

¹O Lᴏʀᴅ, our Lord, how excellent is Your name in all the earth, You who set Your glory above the heavens!

¹O Lᴏʀᴅ, our Lord, how majestic is your name in all the earth! You have set your glory above the heavens.

²Out of the mouth of babes and infants You have ordained strength, because of Your enemies, that You may silence the enemy and the avenger.

²Out of the mouth of babes and infants, you have established strength because of your foes, to still the enemy and the avenger.

³When I consider Your heavens, the work of Your fingers, the moon and the stars, which You have ordained,

³When I look at your heavens, the work of your fingers, the moon and the stars, which you have set in place,

⁴what is man that You are mindful of him, and the son of man that You visit him?

⁴what is man that you are mindful of him, and the son of man that you care for him?

⁵For You have made him a little lower than the angels, and You have crowned him with glory and honor.

⁵Yet you have made him a little lower than the heavenly beings and crowned him with glory and honor.

⁶You have made him to have dominion over the works of Your hands: You have put all

⁶You have given him dominion over the works of your hands; you have put all things

things under his feet,

⁷all sheep and oxen—even the beasts of the field,

⁸the birds of the air, and the fish of the sea that pass through the paths of the seas.

⁹O LORD, our Lord, how excellent is Your name in all the earth! *NKJV*

under his feet,

⁷all sheep and oxen, and also the beasts of the field,

⁸the birds of the heavens, and the fish of the sea, whatever passes along the paths of the seas.

⁹O LORD, our Lord, how majestic is your name in all the earth! *ESV*

Date _____ Parent/Teacher _____

Psalm 119:9, 18, 35

⁹How can a young man cleanse his way? By taking heed according to Your word.

¹⁸Open my eyes, that I may see wondrous things from Your law.

³⁵Make me walk in the path of Your commandments, for I delight in it. *NKJV*

⁹How can a young man keep his way pure? By guarding it according to your word.

¹⁸Open my eyes, that I may behold wondrous things out of your law.

³⁵Lead me in the path of your commandments, for I delight in it. *ESV*

Date _____ Parent/Teacher _____

First Catechism

32. *Q. What does every sin deserve?*
    A. The wrath and curse of God.

33. Q. *What was the sin of our first parents?*
    A. Eating the forbidden fruit.

34. Q. *Who tempted Adam and Eve to this sin?*
    A. Satan tempted Eve first, and then he used her to tempt Adam.

35. Q. *How did Adam and Eve change when they sinned?*
    A. Instead of being holy and happy, they became sinful and miserable.

36. Q. *Did Adam act for himself alone in the covenant of life?*
    A. No. He represented the whole human race.

37. Q. *What effect did the sin of Adam have on you and all people?*
    A. We are all born guilty and sinful.

38. Q. *How sinful are you by nature?*
    A. I am corrupt in every part of my being.

39. Q. *What is the sinful nature that we inherit from Adam called?*
    A. Original sin.

40. Q. *Can anyone go to heaven with this sinful nature?*
    A. No. Our hearts must be changed before we can believe in Jesus and go to heaven.

41. Q. *What is this change of heart called?*
    A. The new birth, or regeneration.

42. Q. *Who can change a sinner's heart?*
    A. The Holy Spirit alone.

43. Q. *Can anyone be saved through the covenant of life?*
    A. No. No one can be saved through the covenant of life.

44. Q. *Why can't anyone be saved through the covenant of life?*
    A. Because all have broken it and are condemned by it.

45. Q. *How did you break the covenant of life?*
    A. Adam represented all people, and so I fell with Adam in his first sin.

46. Q. *How, then, can you be saved?*
    A. By the Lord Jesus Christ through the covenant of grace.

47. Q. *Whom did Christ represent in the covenant of grace?*
    A. His elect people.

48. Q. *How did Christ fulfill the covenant of grace?*
    A. Christ obeyed the whole law for his people, and then suffered the punishment due for their sins.

49. Q. *Did Jesus ever sin?*
    A. No. He lived a sinless life.

50. Q. *How could Christ suffer?*
    A. Christ, the Son of God, became a man so that he could obey and suffer in our place.

51. Q. *For whom did Christ obey and suffer?*
    A. For all whom God the Father gave to Christ.

52. Q. *What kind of life did Christ live on earth?*
    A. A life of obedience, service and suffering.

53. Q. *What kind of death did Jesus die?*
    A. The painful and shameful death of the cross.

54. Q. *What is meant by the atonement?*
    A. Christ satisfied God's justice by his suffering and death as a substitute for sinners.

Date _____ Parent/Teacher _____

Hymns

"All People That on Earth Do Dwell"

Date _____ Parent/Teacher _____

"If with All Your Hearts"

Date _____ Parent/Teacher _____

"When His Salvation Bringing"

Date _____ Parent/Teacher _____

"I Am So Glad"

Date _____ Parent/Teacher _____

"Savior, Teach Me, Day by Day"

Date _____ Parent/Teacher _____

Supplemental Notes

MEMORY WORK

Grade 2

Ten Commandments (shortened)*

1. You shall have no other gods before Me.

2. You shall not make for yourself any carved image.

3. You shall not take the name of the LORD your God in vain.

4. Remember the Sabbath day, to keep it holy.

5. Honor your father and your mother.

6. You shall not murder.

7. You shall not commit adultery.

8. You shall not steal.

9. You shall not bear false witness.

10. You shall not covet.
    NKJV

1. You shall have no other gods before me.

2. You shall not make for yourself a carved image.

3. You shall not take the name of the LORD your God in vain.

4. Remember the Sabbath day, to keep it holy.

5. Honor your father and your mother.

6. You shall not murder.

7. You shall not commit adultery.

8. You shall not steal.

9. You shall not bear false witness.

10. You shall not covet.
    ESV

Date _____ Parent/Teacher _____

*The full version (NKJV) of the Ten Commandments appears on pages 40–43 in *First Catechism* answers.

Mark 16:2-8

²Very early in the morning, on the first day of the week, they came to the tomb when the sun had risen.

³And they said among themselves, "Who will roll away the stone from the door of the tomb for us?"

⁴But when they looked up, they saw that the stone had been rolled away—for it was very large.

⁵And entering the tomb, they saw a young man clothed in a long white robe sitting on the right side; and they were alarmed.

⁶But he said to them, "Do not be alarmed. You seek Jesus of Nazareth, who was crucified. He is risen! He is not here. See the place where they laid Him.

⁷But go and tell His disciples— and Peter—that He is going before you into Galilee; there you will see Him, as He said to you."

⁸And they went out quickly and fled from the tomb, for

²And very early on the first day of the week, when the sun had risen, they went to the tomb.

³And they were saying to one another, "Who will roll away the stone for us from the entrance of the tomb?"

⁴And looking up, they saw that the stone had been rolled back—it was very large.

⁵And entering the tomb, they saw a young man sitting on the right side, dressed in a white robe, and they were alarmed.

⁶And he said to them, "Do not be alarmed. You seek Jesus of Nazareth, who was crucified. He has risen; he is not here. See the place where they laid him.

⁷But go, tell his disciples and Peter that he is going before you to Galilee. There you will see him, just as he told you."

⁸And they went out and fled from the tomb, for trembling and astonishment had seized

they trembled and were amazed. And they said nothing to anyone, for they were afraid. *NKJV*

them, and they said nothing to anyone, for they were afraid. *ESV*

Date _____ Parent/Teacher _____

John 1:14

And the Word became flesh and dwelt among us, and we beheld His glory, the glory as of the only begotten of the Father, full of grace and truth. *NKJV*

And the Word became flesh and dwelt among us, and we have seen his glory, glory as of the only Son from the Father, full of grace and truth. *ESV*

Date _____ Parent/Teacher _____

Psalm 19:1

The heavens declare the glory of God; and the firmament shows His handiwork. *NKJV*

The heavens declare the glory of God, and the sky above proclaims his handiwork. *ESV*

Date _____ Parent/Teacher _____

Psalm 100

[1]Make a joyful shout to the LORD, all you lands!

[1]Make a joyful noise to the LORD, all the earth!

[2]Serve the LORD with gladness; come before His presence with singing.

[2]Serve the LORD with gladness! Come into his presence with singing!

³Know that the LORD, He is God; it is He who has made us, and not we ourselves; we are His people and the sheep of His pasture.

⁴Enter into His gates with thanksgiving, and into His courts with praise. Be thankful to Him and bless His name.

⁵For the LORD is good; His mercy is everlasting, and His truth endures to all generations. *NKJV*

³Know that the LORD, he is God! It is he who made us, and we are his; we are his people, and the sheep of his pasture.

⁴Enter his gates with thanksgiving, and his courts with praise! Give thanks to him; bless his name!

⁵For the LORD is good; his steadfast love endures forever, and his faithfulness to all generations. *ESV*

Date _____ Parent/Teacher _____

First Catechism

55. *Q. What does God the Father guarantee in the covenant of grace?*
    A. To justify and sanctify all those for whom Christ died.

56. *Q. How does God justify you?*
    A. God forgives all my sins and accepts me as righteous through Christ.

57. Q. How does God sanctify you?
    A. God makes me more and more holy in heart and conduct.

58. *Q. What must you do to be saved?*
    A. I must repent of my sin and believe in Christ as my Savior.

59. Q. *How do you repent of your sin?*
    A. I must be sorry for my sin, and hate and forsake it.

60. Q. *Why must you hate and forsake your sin?*
    A. Because sin displeases God.

61. Q. *What does it mean to believe in Christ?*
    A. To trust in Christ alone for my salvation.

62. Q. *Can you repent and believe in Christ by your own power?*
    A. No. I cannot repent and believe unless the Holy Spirit changes my heart.

63. Q. *How can you get the help of the Holy Spirit?*
    A. God has told us to pray for the Holy Spirit's help.

64. Q. *How long ago did Christ die?*
    A. About two thousand years ago.

65. Q. *How were sinners saved before Christ came?*
    A. By believing in the promised Messiah.

66. Q. *Before Christ came, how did believers show their faith?*
    A. By offering the sacrifices God required.

67. Q. *What did these sacrifices represent?*
    A. Christ, the Lamb of God, who would come to die for sinners.

68. Q. *How many offices does Christ fulfill as the promised Messiah?*
    A. Christ fulfills three offices.

69. Q. *What are they?*
    A. The offices of a prophet, of a priest, and of a king.

70. Q. *How is Christ your prophet?*
    A. Christ teaches me the will of God.

71. Q. *How is Christ your priest?*
    A. Christ died for my sins, and continues to pray for me.

72. Q. *How is Christ your king?*
    A. Christ rules over me, the world and Satan, and he defends me.

73. Q. *Why do you need Christ as your prophet?*
    A. Because I am ignorant by nature.

74. Q. *Why do you need Christ as your priest?*
    A. Because I am guilty of breaking God's law.

75. Q. *Why do you need Christ as your king?*
    A. Because I am weak and helpless.

76. Q. *How many commandments did God give on Mount Sinai?*
    A. Ten commandments.

77. Q. *Why should we obey the Ten Commandments?*
    A. Because God is our Creator, Savior and King.

78. Q. *What do the first four commandments teach?*
    A. What it means to love and serve God.

79. Q. *What do the last six commandments teach?*
    A. What it means to love and serve my neighbor.

80. Q. *What do the Ten Commandments teach?*
    A. To love God with all my heart, and my neighbor as myself.

81. Q. *Who is your neighbor?*
    A. Everybody is my neighbor.

82. Q. *Is God pleased with those who love and obey him?*
    A. Yes. God says, "I love them that love me." (KJV)

83. Q. *Is God displeased with those who do not love and obey him?*
    A. Yes. "God is angry with the wicked every day." (KJV)

Date _____ Parent/Teacher _____

Hymns

"Gentle Jesus, Meek and Mild"

Date _____ Parent/Teacher _____

"Love God with All Your Soul"

Date _____ Parent/Teacher _____

"Hosanna, Loud Hosanna"

Date _____ Parent/Teacher _____

Supplemental Notes

MEMORY WORK

Grade 3

Psalm 1

¹Blessed is the man who walks not in the counsel of the ungodly, nor stands in the path of sinners, nor sits in the seat of the scornful;

²But his delight is in the law of the Lord, and in His law he meditates day and night.

³He shall be like a tree planted by the rivers of water that brings forth its fruit in its season, whose leaf also shall not wither; and whatever he does shall prosper.

⁴The ungodly are not so, but are like the chaff which the wind drives away.

⁵Therefore the ungodly shall not stand in the judgment, nor sinners in the congregation of the righteous.

⁶For the Lord knows the way of the righteous, but the way of the ungodly shall perish. *NKJV*

¹Blessed is the man who walks not in the counsel of the wicked, nor stands in the way of sinners, nor sits in the seat of scoffers;

²but his delight is in the law of the Lord, and on his law he meditates day and night.

³He is like a tree planted by streams of water that yields its fruit in its season, and its leaf does not wither. In all that he does, he prospers.

⁴The wicked are not so, but are like chaff that the wind drives away.

⁵Therefore the wicked will not stand in the judgment, nor sinners in the congregation of the righteous;

⁶for the Lord knows the way of the righteous, but the way of the wicked will perish. *ESV*

Date _____ Parent/Teacher _____

37

John 1:1–4

¹In the beginning was the Word, and the Word was with God, and the Word was God.

²He was in the beginning with God.

³All things were made through Him, and without Him nothing was made that was made.

⁴In Him was life, and the life was the light of men. *NKJV*

¹In the beginning was the Word, and the Word was with God, and the Word was God.

²He was in the beginning with God.

³All things were made through him, and without him was not any thing made that was made.

⁴In him was life, and the life was the light of men. *ESV*

Date _____ Parent/Teacher _____

John 11:25, 26

²⁵Jesus said to her, "I am the resurrection and the life. He who believes in Me, though he may die, he shall live.

²⁶And whoever lives and believes in Me shall never die. Do you believe this?" *NKJV*

²⁵Jesus said to her, "I am the resurrection and the life. Whoever believes in me, though he die, yet shall he live,

²⁶and everyone who lives and believes in me shall never die. Do you believe this?" *ESV*

Date _____ Parent/Teacher _____

John 14:1–6

¹"Let not your heart be troubled; you believe in God, believe also in Me.

¹"Let not your hearts be troubled. Believe in God; believe also in me.

2In My Father's house are many mansions; if it were not so, I would have told you. I go to prepare a place for you.

3And if I go and prepare a place for you, I will come again and receive you to Myself; that where I am there you may be also.

4And where I go you know, and the way you know."

5Thomas said to Him, "Lord, we do not know where You are going, and how can we know the way?"

6Jesus said to him, "I am the way, the truth, and the life. No one comes to the Father except through Me." *NKJV*

2In my Father's house are many rooms. If it were not so, would I have told you that I go to prepare a place for you?

3And if I go and prepare a place for you, I will come again and will take you to myself, that where I am you may be also.

4And you know the way to where I am going."

5Thomas said to him, "Lord, we do not know where you are going. How can we know the way?"

6Jesus said to him, "I am the way, and the truth, and the life. No one comes to the Father except through me." *ESV*

Date _____ Parent/Teacher _____

John 5:24

Most assuredly, I say to you, he who hears My word and be-lieves in Him who sent Me has everlasting life, and shall not come into judgment, but has passed from death into life. *NKJV*

Truly, truly, I say to you, whoever hears my word and believes him who sent me has eternal life. He does not come into judgment, but has passed from death to life. *ESV*

Date _____ Parent/Teacher _____

1 John 1:9

If we confess our sins, He is faithful and just to forgive us our sins and to cleanse us from all unrighteousness. *NKJV*

If we confess our sins, he is faithful and just to forgive us our sins and to cleanse us from all unrighteousness. *ESV*

Date _____ Parent/Teacher _____

1 Corinthians 6:19, 20

[19]Or do you not know that your body is the temple of the Holy Spirit who is in you, whom you have from God, and you are not your own?

[20]For you were bought at a price; therefore glorify God in your body and in your spirit, which are God's. *NKJV*

[19]Or do you not know that your body is a temple of the Holy Spirit within you, whom you have from God? You are not your own,

[20]for you were bought with a price. So glorify God in your body. *ESV*

Date _____ Parent/Teacher _____

First Catechism

84. *Q. What is the first commandment?*
    A. The first commandment is "You shall have no other gods before Me." (*NKJV*)

85. *Q. What does the first commandment teach you?*
    A. To worship the true God, and him only.

86. Q. *What is the second commandment?*
    A. The second commandment is "You shall not make for yourself a carved image—any likeness of anything that is in heaven above, or that is in the earth beneath, or that is in the water under the earth; you shall not bow down to them nor serve them. For I, the LORD your God, am a jealous God, visiting the iniquity of the fathers upon the children to the third and fourth generations of those who hate Me, but showing mercy to thousands, to those who love Me and keep My commandments." (*NKJV*)

87. Q. *What does the second commandment teach you?*
    A. To worship God only as he commands, and not to worship God by using statues or pictures.

88. Q. *What is the third commandment?*
    A. The third commandment is "You shall not take the name of the LORD your God in vain, for the LORD will not hold him guiltless who takes His name in vain." (*NKJV*)

89. Q. *What does the third commandment teach you?*
    A. To treat God's name, word and works with reverence.

90. Q. *What is the fourth commandment?*
    A. The fourth commandment is "Remember the Sabbath day, to keep it holy. Six days you shall labor and do all your work, but the seventh day is the Sabbath of the LORD your God. In it you shall do no work: you, nor your son, nor your daughter, nor your male servant, nor your female servant, nor your cattle, nor your stranger who is within your gates. For in six days the LORD made the heavens and the earth, the sea, and all that is in them, and rested the seventh day. Therefore the LORD blessed the Sabbath day and hallowed it." (*NKJV*)

91. Q. *What does the fourth commandment teach you?*
    A. To work six days and keep the Sabbath day holy.

92. Q. *What day of the week is the Christian Sabbath?*
     A. The first day of the week, called the Lord's Day.

93. Q. *Why is it called the Lord's Day?*
     A. Because on that day the Lord Jesus Christ rose from the dead.

94. Q. *How should you keep the Lord's Day?*
     A. I should rest from my daily work and faithfully worship God.

95. Q. *What is the fifth commandment?*
     A. The fifth commandment is "Honor your father and your mother, that your days may be long upon the land which the Lord your God is giving you." (*NKJV*)

96. Q. *What does the fifth commandment teach you?*
     A. To love and obey my parents and all others that God appoints over me.

97. Q. *What is the sixth commandment?*
     A. The sixth commandment is "You shall not murder." (*NKJV*)

98. Q. *What does the sixth commandment teach you?*
     A. Not to take anyone's life unjustly and not to sin when I am angry.

99. Q. *What is the seventh commandment?*
     A. The seventh commandment is "You shall not commit adultery." (*NKJV*)

100. Q. *What does the seventh commandment teach you?*
     A. To be pure in heart, language and conduct, and to be faithful in marriage.

101. *Q.* *What is the eighth commandment?*
    A. The eighth commandment is "You shall not steal." (*NKJV*)

102. *Q.* *What does the eighth commandment teach you?*
    A. Not to take anything that belongs to someone else.

103. *Q.* *What is the ninth commandment?*
    A. The ninth commandment is "You shall not bear false witness against your neighbor." (*NKJV*)

104. *Q.* *What does the ninth commandment teach you?*
    A. Never to lie, but to tell the truth at all times.

105. *Q.* *What is the tenth commandment?*
    A. The tenth commandment is "You shall not covet your neighbor's house; you shall not covet your neighbor's wife, nor his male servant, nor his female servant, nor his ox, nor his donkey, nor anything that is your neighbor's." (*NKJV*)

106. *Q.* *What does the tenth commandment teach you?*
    A. To be content with whatever God chooses to give me.

107. *Q.* *Can you keep the Ten Commandments perfectly?*
    A. No. Since the fall of Adam, the only One who has been able to do this is Jesus.

108. *Q.* *Of what use are the Ten Commandments to you?*
    A. They teach me what is pleasing to God, and how much I need a Savior.

Date _____ Parent/Teacher _____

Grade 3

Hymns

"This Is My Father's World"

Date _____ Parent/Teacher _____

"Gentle Mary Laid Her Child"

Date _____ Parent/Teacher _____

"When He Cometh"

Date _____ Parent/Teacher _____

Supplemental Notes

MEMORY WORK

Grade 4

The Books of the Bible

Old Testament

Genesis	1 Kings	Ecclesiastes	Obadiah
Exodus	2 Kings	Song of Songs	Jonah
Leviticus	1 Chronicles	Isaiah	Micah
Numbers	2 Chronicles	Jeremiah	Nahum
Deuteronomy	Ezra	Lamentations	Habakkuk
Joshua	Nehemiah	Ezekiel	Zephaniah
Judges	Esther	Daniel	Haggai
Ruth	Job	Hosea	Zechariah
1 Samuel	Psalms	Joel	Malachi
2 Samuel	Proverbs	Amos	

Date _____ Parent/Teacher _____

New Testament

Matthew	Ephesians	Hebrews
Mark	Philippians	James
Luke	Colossians	1 Peter
John	1 Thessalonians	2 Peter
Acts	2 Thessalonians	1 John
Romans	1 Timothy	2 John
1 Corinthians	2 Timothy	3 John
2 Corinthians	Titus	Jude
Galatians	Philemon	Revelation

Date _____ Parent/Teacher _____

The Apostles' Creed

I believe in God the Father Almighty, Maker of heaven and earth;

And in Jesus Christ his only Son our Lord; who was conceived by the Holy Ghost; born of the virgin Mary; suffered under Pontius Pilate; was crucified, dead and buried; he descended into hell; the third day he rose again from the dead; he ascended into heaven; and sitteth on the right hand of God the Father Almighty; from thence he shall come to judge the quick and the dead.

I believe in the Holy Ghost, the holy catholic church, the communion of saints, the forgiveness of sins, the resurrection of the body, and the life everlasting. Amen.

Date _____ Parent/Teacher _____

Proverbs 3:5, 6

[5]Trust in the LORD with all your heart, and lean not on your own understanding;

[6]In all you ways acknowledge Him, and he shall direct your paths. *NKJV*

[5]Trust in the LORD with all your heart, and do not lean on your own understanding.

[6]In all your ways acknowledge him, and he will make straight your paths. *ESV*

Date _____ Parent/Teacher _____

1 John 5:4, 5

[4]For whatever is born of God overcomes the world. And this is the victory that has overcome the world—our faith.

[4]For everyone who has been born of God overcomes the world. And this is the victory that has overcome the world—our faith.

⁵Who is he who overcomes the world, but he who believes that Jesus is the Son of God? *NKJV*

⁵Who is it that overcomes the world except the one who believes that Jesus is the Son of God? *ESV*

Date _____ Parent/Teacher _____

Galatians 5:22, 23

²²But the fruit of the Spirit is love, joy, peace, longsuffering, kindness, goodness, faithfulness,

²³gentleness, self-control. Against such there is no law. *NKJV*

²²But the fruit of the Spirit is love, joy, peace, patience, kindness, goodness, faithfulness,

²³gentleness, self-control; against such things there is no law. *ESV*

Date _____ Parent/Teacher _____

Matthew 6:19–21

¹⁹Do not lay up for yourselves treasures on earth, where moth and rust destroy and where thieves break in and steal;

²⁰But lay up for yourselves treasures in heaven where neither moth nor rust destroys and where thieves do not break in and steal.

²¹For where your treasure is,

¹⁹Do not lay up for yourselves treasures on earth, where moth and rust destroy and where thieves break in and steal,

²⁰but lay up for yourselves treasures in heaven, where neither moth nor rust destroys and where thieves do not break in and steal.

²¹For where your treasure is,

there your heart will be also. *NKJV*

there your heart will be also. *ESV*

Date _____ Parent/Teacher _____

Isaiah 12:1, 2

¹And in that day you will say: "O LORD, I will praise You; though You were angry with me, Your anger is turned away, and You comfort me.

²Behold, God is my salvation, I will trust and not be afraid; 'for YAH, the LORD, is my strength and my song; He also has become my salvation.' " *NKJV*

¹You will say in that day: "I will give thanks to you, O LORD, for though you were angry with me, your anger turned away, that you might comfort me.

²"Behold, God is my salvation; I will trust, and will not be afraid; for the LORD GOD is my strength and my song, and he has become my salvation." *ESV*

Date _____ Parent/Teacher _____

John 10:9

I am the door. If anyone enters by Me, he will be saved, and will go in and out and find pasture. *NKJV*

I am the door. If anyone enters by me, he will be saved and will go in and out and find pasture. *ESV*

Date _____ Parent/Teacher _____

Revelation 15:3b, 4

Great and marvelous are Your

Great and amazing are your

works,
  Lord God Almighty!
Just and true are Your ways,
  O King of the saints!
Who shall not fear You, O
  Lord,
  and glorify Your name?
For You alone are holy.
For all nations shall come
  and worship before You.
For Your judgments have
  been manifested. *NKJV*

deeds,
  O Lord God the Almighty!
Just and true are your
  ways,
  O King of the nations!
Who will not fear, O Lord,
  and glorify your name?
For you alone are holy.
  All nations will come
  and worship you,
for your righteous acts have
  been revealed. *ESV*

Date _____ Parent/Teacher _____

First Catechism

109. Q. *What is prayer?*
   A. Prayer is praising God, giving thanks for all his bless-
       ings, and asking him for the things he has promised
       in the Bible.

110. Q. *In whose name should we pray?*
   A. Only in the name of Christ.

111. Q. *What did Christ give us to teach us about prayer?*
   A. The Lord's Prayer.

112. Q. *What is the Lord's Prayer?*
   A. The Lord's Prayer is "Our Father which art in heaven,
       Hallowed be thy name. Thy kingdom come. Thy will be
       done in earth, as it is in heaven. Give us this day our
       daily bread. And forgive us our debts, as we forgive
       our debtors. And lead us not into temptation, but
       deliver us from evil: For thine is the kingdom, and
       the power, and the glory, for ever. Amen." (KJV)

113. Q. *How many petitions are there in the Lord's Prayer?*
     A. Six.

114. Q. *What is the first petition?*
     A. The first petition is "Hallowed be thy name."

115. Q. *What does it mean to pray, "Hallowed be thy name"?*
     A. We are asking God to help us and others to respect and honor him.

116. Q. *What is the second petition?*
     A. The second petition is "Thy kingdom come."

117. Q. *What does it mean to pray, "Thy kingdom come"?*
     A. We are asking God to bring more and more people to hear, believe and obey his gospel.

118. Q. *What is the third petition?*
     A. The third petition is "Thy will be done in earth, as it is in heaven."

119. Q. *What does it mean to pray, "Thy will be done in earth, as it is in heaven"?*
     A. We are asking God to make us able and willing to serve him on earth just as he is served in heaven.

120. Q. *What is the fourth petition?*
     A. The fourth petition is "Give us this day our daily bread."

121. Q. *What does it mean to pray, "Give us this day our daily bread"?*
     A. We are asking God to provide us with all that we really need.

122. Q. *What is the fifth petition?*
     A. The fifth petition is "And forgive us our debts, as we forgive our debtors."

123. Q. *What does it mean to pray, "And forgive us our debts, as we forgive our debtors"?*
A. We are asking God to forgive our sins for Christ's sake, and to make us willing to forgive others.

124. Q. *What is the sixth petition?*
A. The sixth petition is "And lead us not into temptation, but deliver us from evil."

125. Q. *What does it mean to pray, "And lead us not into temptation, but deliver us from evil"?*
A. We are asking God to keep us from being tempted and to make us strong enough to resist when we are tempted.

126. Q. How many sacraments are there?
A. Two.

127. Q. *What are they?*
A. Baptism and the Lord's Supper.

128. Q. *Who appointed these sacraments?*
A. The Lord Jesus Christ.

129. Q. *Why did Christ appoint these sacraments?*
A. To distinguish his people from the world, and to comfort and strengthen them.

130. Q. *What sign is used in baptism?*
A. Washing with water.

131. Q. *What does this washing with water represent?*
A. That we are united to Christ and cleansed from sin by his blood.

132. Q. *Into whose name are we baptized?*
A. Into the name of the Father, and of the Son and of the Holy Spirit.

133. *Q.* *Who are to be baptized?*
     A.   Believers and their children.

134. *Q.* *Why are we baptized even as little infants?*
     A.   Because God includes the children of believers in his covenant and marks them in baptism.

135. *Q.* *What did Jesus say about little children?*
     A.   "Let the little children come to me, and do not hinder them, for the kingdom of heaven belongs to such as these."

136. *Q.* *What does baptism call you to be?*
     A.   A true follower of Christ.

137. *Q.* *What sign is used in the Lord's Supper?*
     A.   Eating bread and drinking wine to remember the suffering and death of Jesus.

138. *Q.* *What does the bread represent?*
     A.   Christ's body sacrificed for our sins.

139. *Q.* *What does the wine represent?*
     A.   Christ's blood shed for our sins.

140. *Q.* *Who may rightly partake of the Lord's Supper?*
     A.   Those who repent of their sins, trust in Christ, live a godly life, and profess their faith before the Church.

141. *Q.* *Did Christ remain in the grave after his crucifixion?*
     A.   No. He rose bodily from the grave on the third day after his death.

142. *Q.* *Where is Christ now?*
     A.   In heaven, ruling his kingdom and interceding for us.

143. *Q.* *Will the Lord Jesus come again?*
     A.   Yes! He will return to judge the world on the last day.

144. Q. *What happens to believers when they die?*
    A. Our bodies will return to the dust and our souls will go to be with the Lord forever.

145. Q. *What happens to unbelievers when they die?*
    A. Their bodies will return to dust also, but their souls will go to hell.

146. Q. *What is hell?*
    A. Hell is an awful place, where unbelievers are separated from God to suffer for their sins.

147. Q. *Will the bodies of all the dead be raised again?*
    A. Yes. At the last day some will be raised to everlasting life and others to everlasting death.

148. Q. *What will God do to unbelievers at the last day?*
    A. He will judge them, and condemn them to everlasting punishment in the lake of fire with Satan and his angels.

149. Q. *What will God do for believers at the last day?*
    A. He will give them a home with him in the new heaven and the new earth.

150. Q. *What will the new heaven and the new earth be like?*
    A. A glorious and happy place, where the saved will be with Jesus forever.

Date _____ Parent/Teacher _____

Hymns

"Stand Up, Stand Up for Jesus"

Date _____ Parent/Teacher _____

Grade 4

"Come, Holy Spirit, Come"

Date _____ Parent/Teacher _____

"There Is No Name So Sweet on Earth"

Date _____ Parent/Teacher _____

"Yield Not to Temptation"

Date _____ Parent/Teacher _____

Supplemental Notes

MEMORY WORK

Grade 5

Psalm 103:1–8

[1]Bless the LORD, O my soul; and all that is within me, bless His holy name!

[2]Bless the LORD, O my soul, and forget not all His benefits:

[3]Who forgives all your iniquities, who heals all your diseases,

[4]Who redeems your life from destruction, who crowns you with lovingkindness and tender mercies,

[5]Who satisfies your mouth with good things, so that your youth is renewed like the eagle's.

[6]The LORD executes righteousness and justice for all who are oppressed.

[7]He made known His ways to Moses, His acts to the children of Israel.

[8]The LORD is merciful and gracious, slow to anger, and abounding in mercy. *NKJV*

[1]Bless the LORD, O my soul, and all that is within me, bless his holy name!

[2]Bless the LORD, O my soul, and forget not all his benefits,

[3]who forgives all your iniquity, who heals all your diseases,

[4]who redeems your life from the pit, who crowns you with steadfast love and mercy,

[5]who satisfies you with good so that your youth is renewed like the eagle's.

[6]The LORD works righteousness and justice for all who are oppressed.

[7]He made known his ways to Moses, his acts to the people of Israel.

[8]The LORD is merciful and gracious, slow to anger and abounding in steadfast love. *ESV*

Date _____ Parent/Teacher _____

Isaiah 46:9, 10

⁹ Remember the former things of old, for I am God, and there is no other; I am God, and there is none like Me,

¹⁰declaring the end from the beginning, and from ancient times things that are not yet done, saying, "My counsel shall stand, and I will do all My pleasure." *NKJV*

⁹ Remember the former things of old; for I am God, and there is no other; I am God, and there is none like me,

¹⁰declaring the end from the beginning and from ancient times things not yet done, saying, "My counsel shall stand, and I will accomplish all my purpose." *ESV*

Date _____ Parent/Teacher _____

Deuteronomy 29:29

The secret things belong to the Lᴏʀᴅ our God, but those things which are revealed belong to us and to our children forever, that we may do all the words of this law. *NKJV*

The secret things belong to the Lᴏʀᴅ our God, but the things that are revealed belong to us and to our children forever, that we may do all the words of this law. *ESV*

Date _____ Parent/Teacher _____

Ten Commandments (Exodus 20:3–17)*

1. You shall have no other

1. You shall have no other

*The Ten Commandments also appear in the Shorter Catechism on pages 74–78 and 82–83.

gods before Me.

2. You shall not make for yourself any carved image, or any likeness of anything that is in heaven above, or that is in the earth beneath, or that is in the water under the earth; you shall not bow down to them nor serve them. For I, the LORD your God, am a jealous God, visiting the iniquity of the fathers on the children to the third and fourth generations of those who hate Me, but showing mercy to thousands, to those who love Me and keep My commandments.

3. You shall not take the name of the LORD your God in vain, for the LORD will not hold him guiltless who takes His name in vain.

4. Remember the Sabbath day, to keep it holy. Six days you shall labor and do all your work, but the seventh day is the Sabbath of the LORD your God. In it you shall do no work: you, nor your son, nor your daughter, nor your manservant, nor your maidservant, nor your cattle, nor your stranger who is within your gates. For in six days the LORD made the heavens and the earth, the sea, and

gods before me.

2. You shall not make for yourself a carved image, or any likeness of anything that is in heaven above, or that is in the earth beneath, or that is in the water under the earth. You shall not bow down to them or serve them, for I the LORD your God am a jealous God, visiting the iniquity of the fathers on the children to the third and the fourth generation of those who hate me, but showing steadfast love to thousands of those who love me and keep my commandments.

3. You shall not take the name of the LORD your God in vain, for the LORD will not hold him guiltless who takes his name in vain.

4. Remember the Sabbath day, to keep it holy. Six days you shall labor, and do all your work, but the seventh day is a Sabbath to the LORD your God. On it you shall not do any work, you, or your son, or your daughter, your male servant, or your female servant, or your livestock, or the sojourner who is within your gates. For in six days the LORD made heaven and earth, the sea, and all that is

all that is in them, and rested the seventh day. Therefore the LORD blessed the Sabbath day and hallowed it.

5. Honor your father and your mother, that your days may be long upon the land which the LORD your God is giving you.

6. You shall not murder.

7. You shall not commit adultery.

8. You shall not steal.

9. You shall not bear false witness against your neighbor.

10. You shall not covet your neighbor's house; you shall not covet your neighbor's wife, nor his manservant, nor his maidservant, nor his ox, nor his donkey, nor anything that is your neighbor's. *NKJV*

in them, and rested the seventh day. Therefore the LORD blessed the Sabbath day and made it holy.

5. Honor your father and your mother, that your days may be long in the land that the LORD your God is giving you.

6. You shall not murder.

7. You shall not commit adultery.

8. You shall not steal.

9. You shall not bear false witness against your neighbor.

10. You shall not covet your neighbor's house; you shall not covet your neighbor's wife, or his male servant, or his female servant, or his ox, or his donkey, or anything that is your neighbor's. *ESV*

Date _____ Parent/Teacher _____

Beatitudes (Matthew 5:3–12)

Blessed are the poor in spirit,   Blessed are the poor in spirit, for theirs is the kingdom of heaven.

Blessed are those who mourn, for they shall be comforted.

Blessed are the meek, for they shall inherit the earth.

Blessed are those who hunger and thirst for righteousness, for they shall be filled.

Blessed are the merciful, for they shall obtain mercy.

Blessed are the pure in heart, for they shall see God.

Blessed are the peacemakers, for they shall be called sons of God.

Blessed are those who are persecuted for righteousness sake, for theirs is the kingdom of heaven.

Blessed are you when they revile and persecute you, and say all kinds of evil against you falsely for My sake.

Rejoice and be exceedingly glad, for great is your reward in heaven, for so they persecuted the prophets who were

for theirs is the kingdom of heaven.

Blessed are those who mourn, for they will be comforted.

Blessed are the meek, for they will inherit the earth.

Blessed are those who hunger and thirst for righteousness, for they will be filled.

Blessed are the merciful, for they will be shown mercy.

Blessed are the pure in heart, for they will see God.

Blessed are the peacemakers, for they will be called sons of God.

Blessed are those who are persecuted because of right-eousness, for theirs is the kingdom of heaven.

Blessed are you when people insult you, persecute you and falsely say all kinds of evil against you because of me.

Rejoice and be glad, because great is your reward in heaven, for in the same way they per-secuted the prophets who were before you. *NKJV*   before you. *ESV*

Date _____ Parent/Teacher _____

Ephesians 1:2–9

[2]Grace to you and peace from God our Father and the Lord Jesus Christ.

[3]Blessed be the God and Father of our Lord Jesus Christ, who has blessed us with every spiritual blessing in the heavenly places in Christ,

[4]just as He chose us in Him before the foundation of the world, that we should be holy and without blame before Him in love,

[5]having predestined us to adoption as sons by Jesus Christ to Himself, according to the good pleasure of His will,

[6]to the praise of the glory of His grace, by which He has made us accepted in the Beloved.

[7]In Him we have redemption through His blood, the forgiveness of sins, according to the riches of His grace

[2]Grace to you and peace from God our Father and the Lord Jesus Christ.

[3]Blessed be the God and Father of our Lord Jesus Christ, who has blessed us in Christ with every spiritual blessing in the heavenly places,

[4]even as he chose us in him before the foundation of the world, that we should be holy and blameless before him. In love

[5]he predestined us for adoption through Jesus Christ, according to the purpose of his will,

[6]to the praise of his glorious grace, with which he has blessed us in the Beloved.

[7]In him we have redemption through his blood, the forgiveness of our trespasses, according to the riches of his grace,

⁸which He made to abound toward us in all wisdom and prudence,

⁹having made known to us the mystery of His will, according to His good pleasure which He purposed in Himself. *NKJV*

⁸which he lavished upon us, in all wisdom and insight

⁹making known to us the mystery of his will, according to his purpose, which he set forth in Christ. *ESV*

Date _____ Parent/Teacher _____

Shorter Catechism

1. *Q. What is the chief end of man?*
   A. Man's chief end is to glorify God and to enjoy him forever.

2. *Q. What rule has God given to direct us how we may glorify and enjoy him?*
   A. The Word of God, which is contained in the Scriptures of the Old and New Testaments, is the only rule to direct us how we may glorify and enjoy him.

3. *Q. What do the Scriptures principally teach?*
   A. The Scriptures principally teach what man is to believe concerning God, and what duty God requires of man.

4. *Q. What is God?*
   A. God is a Spirit, infinite, eternal, and unchangeable in his being, wisdom, power, holiness, justice, goodness and truth.

5. *Q. Are there more Gods than one?*
   A. There is but one only, the living and true God.

6. *Q. How many persons are there in the Godhead?*
   A. There are three persons in the Godhead: the Father, the

Son, and the Holy Spirit; and these three are one God, the same in substance, equal in power and glory.

7. *Q. What are the decrees of God?*
   A. The decrees of God are his eternal purpose according to the counsel of his will, whereby, for his own glory, he has foreordained whatsoever comes to pass.

8. *Q. How does God execute his decrees?*
   A. God executes his decrees in the works of creation and providence.

9. *Q. What is the work of creation?*
   A. The work of creation is God's making all things of nothing by the word of his power in the space of six days—and all very good.

10. *Q. How did God create man?*
    A. God created man, male and female, after his own image in knowledge, righteousness and holiness, with dominion over the creatures.

11. *Q. What are God's works of providence?*
    A. God's works of providence are his most holy, wise and powerful preserving and governing all his creatures and all their actions.

12. *Q. What special act of providence did God exercise towards man in the estate wherein he was created?*
    A. When God had created man, he entered into a covenant of life with him upon condition of perfect obedience, forbidding him to eat of the tree of the knowledge of good and evil upon pain of death.

13. *Q. Did our first parents continue in the estate wherein they were created?*
    A. Our first parents, being left to the freedom of their own

will, fell from the estate wherein they were created, by sinning against God.

14. *Q. What is sin?*
    A. Sin is any want of conformity unto, or transgression of, the law of God.

15. *Q. What was the sin whereby our first parents fell from the estate wherein they were created?*
    A. The sin whereby our first parents fell from the estate wherein they were created, was their eating the forbidden fruit.

16. *Q. Did all mankind fall in Adam's first transgression?*
    A. The covenant being made with Adam not only for himself but for his posterity, all mankind descending from him by ordinary generation sinned in him and fell with him in his first transgression.

17. *Q. Into what estate did the fall bring mankind?*
    A. The fall brought mankind into an estate of sin and misery.

18. *Q. Wherein consists the sinfulness of that estate whereinto man fell?*
    A. The sinfulness of that estate whereinto man fell consists in the guilt of Adam's first sin, the want of original righteousness and the corruption of his whole nature, which is commonly called original sin, together with all actual transgressions which proceed from it.

19. *Q. What is the misery of that estate whereinto man fell?*
    A. All mankind by their fall lost communion with God, are under his wrath and curse, and so are made liable to all miseries in this life, to death itself and to the pains of hell forever.

20. Q. *Did God leave all mankind to perish in the estate of sin and misery?*
    A. God, having out of his mere good pleasure from all eternity elected some to everlasting life, did enter into a covenant of grace to deliver them out of the estate of sin and misery, and to bring them into an estate of salvation by a Redeemer.

21. Q. *Who is the Redeemer of God's elect?*
    A. The only Redeemer of God's elect is the Lord Jesus Christ, who, being the eternal Son of God, became man and so was and continues to be God and man in two distinct natures and one person forever.

22. Q. *How did Christ, being the Son of God, become man?*
    A. Christ, the Son of God, became man by taking to himself a true body and a reasonable soul, being conceived by the power of the Holy Spirit in the womb of the virgin Mary and born of her, yet without sin.

23. Q. *What offices does Christ execute as our Redeemer?*
    A. Christ, as our Redeemer, executes the offices of a prophet, of a priest and of a king, both in his estate of humiliation and exaltation.

24. Q. *How does Christ execute the office of a prophet?*
    A. Christ executes the office of a prophet in revealing to us by his Word and Spirit the will of God for our salvation.

25. Q. *How does Christ execute the office of a priest?*
    A. Christ executes the office of a priest in his once offering up of himself a sacrifice to satisfy divine justice and reconcile us to God, and in making continual intercession for us.

26. Q. *How does Christ execute the office of a king?*
    A. Christ executes the office of a king in subduing us to

himself, in ruling and defending us and in restraining and conquering all his and our enemies.

27. Q. *Wherein did Christ's humiliation consist?*
    A. Christ's humiliation consisted in his being born (and that in a low condition), made under the law, undergoing the miseries of this life, the wrath of God and the cursed death of the cross, in being buried and continuing under the power of death for a time.

28. Q. *Wherein consists Christ's exaltation?*
    A. Christ's exaltation consists in his rising again from the dead on the third day, in ascending up into heaven, in sitting at the right hand of God the Father and in coming to judge the world at the last day.

29. Q. *How are we made partakers of the redemption purchased by Christ?*
    A. We are made partakers of the redemption purchased by Christ by the effectual application of it to us by his Holy Spirit.

30. Q. *How does the Spirit apply to us the redemption purchased by Christ?*
    A. The Spirit applies to us the redemption purchased by Christ by working faith in us, and thereby uniting us to Christ in our effectual calling.

31. Q. *What is effectual calling?*
    A. Effectual calling is the work of God's Spirit, whereby, convincing us of our sin and misery, enlightening our minds in the knowledge of Christ and renewing our wills, he persuades and enables us to embrace Jesus Christ freely offered to us in the gospel.

32. Q. *What benefits do they that are effectually called partake of in this life?*

65

A. They that are effectually called do in this life partake of justification, adoption and sanctification, and the several benefits which in this life do either accompany or flow from them.

33. *Q. What is justification?*
A. Justification is an act of God's free grace, wherein he pardons all our sins and accepts us as righteous in his sight, only for the righteousness of Christ, imputed to us, and received by faith alone.

34. *Q. What is adoption?*
A. Adoption is an act of God's free grace, whereby we are received into the number, and have a right to all the privileges, of the sons of God.

35. *Q. What is sanctification?*
A. Sanctification is the work of God's free grace, whereby we are renewed in the whole man after the image of God and are enabled more and more to die unto sin and live unto righteousness.

Date _____ Parent/Teacher _____

Hymns

"Onward, Christian Soldiers"

Date _____ Parent/Teacher _____

"Christ the Lord Is Risen Today"

Date _____ Parent/Teacher _____

"Thy Word Have I Hid in My Heart"

Date _____ Parent/Teacher _____

"Sound the Battle Cry!"

Date _____ Parent/Teacher _____

Supplemental Notes

MEMORY WORK

Grade 6

1 Corinthians 13

¹Though I speak with the tongues of men and of angels, but have not love, I have become as sounding brass or a clanging cymbal.

²And though I have the gift of prophecy, and understand all mysteries and all knowledge, and though I have all faith, so that I could remove mountains, but have not love, I am nothing.

³And though I bestow all my goods to feed the poor, and though I give my body to be burned, but have not love, it profits me nothing.

⁴Love suffers long and is kind; love does not envy; love does not parade itself, is not puffed up;

⁵does not behave rudely, does not seek its own, is not provoked, thinks no evil;

⁶does not rejoice in iniquity, but rejoices in the truth;

¹If I speak in the tongues of men and of angels, but have not love, I am a noisy gong or a clanging cymbal.

²And if I have prophetic powers, and understand all mysteries and all knowledge, and if I have all faith, so as to remove mountains, but have not love, I am nothing.

³If I give away all I have, and if I deliver up my body to be burned, but have not love, I gain nothing.

⁴Love is patient and kind; love does not envy or boast; it is not arrogant

⁵or rude. It does not insist on its own way; it is not irritable or resentful;

⁶it does not rejoice at wrongdoing, but rejoices with the truth.

⁷Love bears all things, believes all things, hopes all things,

⁷bears all things, believes all things, hopes all things, endures all things.

⁸Love never fails. But whether there are prophecies, they will fail; whether there are tongues, they will cease; whether there is knowledge, it will vanish away.

⁹For we know in part and we prophesy in part.

¹⁰But when that which is perfect has come, then that which is in part will be done away.

¹¹When I was a child, I spoke as a child, I understood as a child, I thought as a child; but when I became a man, I put away childish things.

¹²For now we see in a mirror, dimly, but then face to face. Now I know in part, but then I shall know just as I also am known.

¹³And now abide faith, hope, love, these three; but the greatest of these is love. *NKJV*

endures all things.

⁸Love never ends. As for prophecies, they will pass away; as for tongues, they will cease; as for knowledge, it will pass away.

⁹For we know in part and we prophesy in part,

¹⁰but when the perfect comes, the partial will pass away.

¹¹When I was a child, I spoke like a child, I thought like a child, I reasoned like a child. When I became a man, I gave up childish ways.

¹²For now we see in a mirror dimly, but then face to face. Now I know in part; then I shall know fully, even as I have been fully known.

¹³So now faith, hope, and love abide, these three; but the greatest of these is love. *ESV*

Date _____ Parent/Teacher _____

Isaiah 40:25–31

²⁵"To whom then will you liken Me, or to whom shall I be equal?" says the Holy One.

²⁶Lift up your eyes on high, and see who has created these things, who brings out their host by number; He calls them all by name, by the greatness of His might and the strength of His power; not one is missing.

²⁷Why do you say, O Jacob, and speak, O Israel: "My way is hidden from the Lord, and my just claim is passed over by my God"?

²⁸Have you not known? Have you not heard? The everlasting God, the Lord, the Creator of the ends of the earth, neither faints nor is weary. His understanding is unsearchable.

²⁹He gives power to the weak, and to those who have no might He increases strength.

³⁰Even the youths shall faint and be weary, and the young men shall utterly fall,

³¹but those who wait on the Lord shall renew their strength; they shall mount up with wings like eagles, they shall run and not be weary, they shall walk and not faint. *NKJV*

²⁵To whom then will you compare me, that I should be like him? says the Holy One.

²⁶Lift up your eyes on high and see: who created these? He who brings out their host by number, calling them all by name, by the greatness of his might, and because he is strong in power not one is missing.

²⁷Why do you say, O Jacob, and speak, O Israel, "My way is hidden from the Lord, and my right is disregarded by my God"?

²⁸Have you not known? Have you not heard? The Lord is the everlasting God, the Creator of the ends of the earth. He does not faint or grow weary; his understanding is unsearchable.

²⁹He gives power to the faint, and to him who has no might he increases strength.

³⁰Even youths shall faint and be weary, and young men shall fall exhausted;

³¹but they who wait for the Lord shall renew their strength; they shall mount up with wings like eagles; they shall run and not be weary; they shall walk and not faint. *ESV*

Date _____ Parent/Teacher _____

Matthew 22:36–40

[36]"Teacher, which is the great commandment in the law?"

[37]Jesus said to him, "You shall love the Lord your God with all your heart, with all your soul, and with all your mind.'

[38]This is the first and great commandment.

[39]And the second is like it: 'You shall love your neighbor as yourself.'

[40]On these two commandments hang all the Law and the Prophets." *NKJV*

[36]"Teacher, which is the great commandment in the Law?"

[37]And he said to him, "You shall love the Lord your God with all your heart and with all your soul and with all your mind.

[38]This is the great and first commandment.

[39] And a second is like it: You shall love your neighbor as yourself.

[40]On these two commandments depend all the Law and the Prophets." *ESV*

Date _____ Parent/Teacher _____

Mark 10:45

For even the Son of Man did not come to be served, but to serve, and to give His life a ransom for many. *NKJV*

For even the Son of Man came not to be served but to serve, and to give his life as a ransom for many. *ESV*

Date _____ Parent/Teacher _____

Shorter Catechism

36. *Q. What are the benefits which in this life do accompany or flow from justification, adoption and sanctification?*
 A. The benefits which in this life do accompany or flow from justification, adoption and sanctification are assurance of God's love, peace of conscience, joy in the Holy Spirit, increase of grace, and perseverance therein to the end.

37. *Q. What benefits do believers receive from Christ at death?*
 A. The souls of believers are at their death made perfect in holiness and do immediately pass into glory; and their bodies, being still united to Christ, do rest in their graves until the resurrection.

38. *Q. What benefits do believers receive from Christ at the resurrection?*
 A. At the resurrection believers, being raised up in glory, shall be openly acknowledged and acquitted in the day of judgment and made perfectly blessed in the full enjoying of God to all eternity.

39. *Q. What is the duty which God requires of man?*
 A. The duty which God requires of man is obedience to his revealed will.

40. *Q. What did God at first reveal to man for the rule of his obedience?*
 A. The rule which God at first revealed to man for his obedience was the moral law.

41. *Q. Wherein is the moral law summarily comprehended?*
 A. The moral law is summarily comprehended in the Ten Commandments.

42. *Q. What is the sum of the Ten Commandments?*
 A. The sum of the Ten Commandments is to love the Lord

our God with all our heart, with all our soul, with all our strength and with all our mind, and our neighbor as ourselves.

43. Q. What is the preface to the Ten Commandments?
    A. The preface to the Ten Commandments is in these words, "I am the LORD your God, who brought you out of Egypt, out of the land of slavery."

44. Q. What does the preface to the Ten Commandments teach us?
    A. The preface to the Ten Commandments teaches us that because God is the Lord, and our God, and Redeemer, therefore we are bound to keep all his commandments.

45. Q. Which is the first commandment?
    A. The first commandment is, "You shall have no other gods before me."

46. Q. What is required in the first commandment?
    A. The first commandment requires us to know and acknowledge God to be the only true God and our God, and to worship and glorify him accordingly.

47. Q. What is forbidden in the first commandment?
    A. The first commandment forbids the denying, or not worshiping and glorifying, the true God as God and our God and the giving of that worship and glory to any other, which is due to him alone.

48. Q. What are we especially taught by these words, "before me," in the first commandment?
    A. These words, "before me," in the first commandment teach us that God, who sees all things, takes notice of—and is much displeased with—the sin of having any other god.

49. *Q. Which is the second commandment?*
   A. The second commandment is, "You shall not make for yourself an idol in the form of anything in heaven above or on the earth beneath or in the waters below. You shall not bow down to them or worship them; for I, the LORD your God, am a jealous God, punishing the children for the sin of fathers to the third and fourth generation of those who hate me, but showing love to thousands who love me and keep my commands."

50. *Q. What is required in the second commandment?*
   A. The second commandment requires the receiving, observing and keeping pure and entire, all such religious worship and ordinances as God has appointed in his Word.

51. *Q. What is forbidden in the second commandment?*
   A. The second commandment forbids the worshiping of God by images or any other way not appointed in his Word.

52. *Q. What are the reasons annexed to the second commandment?*
   A. The reasons annexed to the second commandment are God's sovereignty over us, his propriety in us and the zeal he has for his own worship.

53. *Q. Which is the third commandment?*
   A. The third commandment is, "You shall not misuse the name of the LORD your God, for the LORD will not hold anyone guiltless who misuses his name."

54. *Q. What is required in the third commandment?*
   A. The third commandment requires the holy and reverent use of God's names, titles, attributes, ordinances, Word and works.

55. *Q. What is forbidden in the third commandment?*
    A. The third commandment forbids all profaning or abus-
       ing of anything whereby God makes himself known.

56. *Q. What is the reason annexed to the third commandment?*
    A. The reason annexed to the third commandment is that
       however the breakers of this commandment may escape
       punishment from men, yet the Lord our God will not
       allow them to escape his righteous judgment.

57. *Q. Which is the fourth commandment?*
    A. The fourth commandment is, "Remember the Sabbath
       day by keeping it holy. Six days you shall labor and do
       all your work, but the seventh day is a Sabbath to the
       LORD your God. On it you shall not do any work, neither
       you, nor your son or daughter, nor your manservant or
       maidservant, nor your animals, nor the alien within
       your gates. For in six days the LORD made the heavens
       and the earth, the sea, and all that is in them, but he
       rested on the seventh day. Therefore the LORD blessed
       the Sabbath day and made it holy."

58. *Q. What is required in the fourth commandment?*
    A. The fourth commandment requires the keeping holy to
       God such set times as he has appointed in his Word,
       expressly one whole day in seven, to be a holy Sabbath
       to himself.

59. *Q. Which day of the seven has God appointed to be the
    weekly Sabbath?*
    A. From the beginning of the world to the resurrection of
       Christ, God appointed the seventh day of the week to be
       the weekly Sabbath, and the first day of the week, ever
       since, to continue to the end of the world, which is the
       Christian Sabbath.

60. *Q. How is the Sabbath to be sanctified?*

A. The Sabbath is to be sanctified by a holy resting all that day, even from such worldly employments and recreations as are lawful on other days; and spending the whole time in the public and private exercises of God's worship, except so much as is to be taken up in works of necessity and mercy.

61. Q. *What is forbidden in the fourth commandment?*
A. The fourth commandment forbids the omission or careless performance of the duties required, and the profaning the day by idleness, or doing that which is in itself sinful, or by unnecessary thoughts, words or works about our worldly employments or recreations.

62. Q. *What are the reasons annexed to the fourth commandment?*
A. The reasons annexed to the fourth commandment are God's allowing us six days of the week for our own employments, his challenging a special propriety in the seventh, his own example and his blessing the Sabbath day.

63. Q. *Which is the fifth commandment?*
A. The fifth commandment is, "Honor your father and your mother, so that you may live long in the land the LORD your God is giving you."

64. Q. *What is required in the fifth commandment?*
A. The fifth commandment requires the preserving the honor and performing the duties belonging to everyone in their several places and relations, as superiors, inferiors or equals.

65. Q. *What is forbidden in the fifth commandment?*
A. The fifth commandment forbids the neglecting of, or doing anything against, the honor and duty which belongs to everyone in their several places and relations.

66. Q. *What is the reason annexed to the fifth commandment?*
    A. The reason annexed to the fifth commandment is a promise of long life and prosperity (as far as it shall serve for God's glory, and their own good) to all who keep this commandment.

67. Q. *Which is the sixth commandment?*
    A. The sixth commandment is, "You shall not murder."

68. Q. *What is required in the sixth commandment?*
    A. The sixth commandment requires all lawful endeavors to preserve our own life and the life of others.

69. Q. *What is forbidden in the sixth commandment?*
    A. The sixth commandment forbids the taking away of our own life or the life of our neighbor unjustly, or whatsoever tends thereunto.

Date _____ Parent/Teacher _____

Hymns

"More about Jesus"

Date _____ Parent/Teacher _____

"What Can Wash Away My Sin?"

Date _____ Parent/Teacher _____

"Bring Them In"

Date _____ Parent/Teacher _____

"Dare to Be a Daniel!"

Date _____ Parent/Teacher _____

MEMORY WORK

Grade 7

Read the Gospel of Matthew

Date _____ Parent/Teacher _____

John 15:16

You did not choose Me, but I chose you and appointed you that you should go and bear fruit, and that your fruit should remain, that whatever you ask the Father in My name He may give you. *NKJV*

You did not choose me, but I chose you and appointed you that you should go and bear fruit and that your fruit should abide, so that whatever you ask the Father in my name, he may give it to you. *ESV*

Date _____ Parent/Teacher _____

John 17:9–11

[9]I pray for them. I do not pray for the world but for those whom You have given Me, for they are Yours.

[10]And all Mine are Yours, and Yours are Mine, and I am glorified in them.

[11]Now I am no longer in the world, but these are in the world, and I come to You. Holy

[9]I am praying for them. I am not praying for the world but for those whom you have given me, for they are yours.

[10]All mine are yours, and yours are mine, and I am glorified in them.

[11]And I am no longer in the world, but they are in the world, and I am coming to

Father, keep through Your name those who You have given Me, that they may be one as We are. *NKJV*

you. Holy Father, keep them in your name, which you have given me, that they may be one, even as we are one. *ESV*

Date _____ Parent/Teacher _____

Psalm 27

¹The LORD is my light and my salvation; whom shall I fear? The LORD is the strength of my life; of whom shall I be afraid?

²When the wicked came against me to eat up my flesh, my enemies and foes, they stumbled and fell.

³Though an army should encamp against me, my heart shall not fear; though war should rise against me, in this I will be confident.

⁴One thing I have desired of the LORD, that will I seek: that I may dwell in the house of the LORD all the days of my life, to behold the beauty of the LORD, and to inquire in His temple.

⁵For in the time of trouble He shall hide me in His pavilion; in the secret place of His tab-

¹The LORD is my light and my salvation; whom shall I fear? The LORD is the stronghold of my life; of whom shall I be afraid?

²When evildoers assail me to eat up my flesh, my adversaries and foes, it is they who stumble and fall.

³Though an army encamp against me, my heart shall not fear; though war arise against me, yet I will be confident.

⁴One thing have I asked of the LORD, that will I seek after: that I may dwell in the house of the LORD all the days of my life, to gaze upon the beauty of the LORD and to inquire in his temple.

⁵For he will hide me in his shelter in the day of trouble; he

ernacle He shall hide me; He shall set me high upon a rock.

⁶And now my head shall be lifted up above my enemies all around me; therefore I will offer sacrifices of joy in His tabernacle; I will sing, yes, I will sing praises to the LORD.

⁷Hear, O LORD, when I cry with my voice! Have mercy also upon me, and answer me.

⁸When You said, "Seek My face," my heart said to You, "Your face, LORD, I will seek."

⁹Do not hide Your face from me; do not turn Your servant away in anger; You have been my help; do not leave me nor forsake me, O God of my salvation.

¹⁰When my father and my mother forsake me, then the LORD will take care of me.

¹¹Teach me Your way, O LORD, and lead me in a smooth path, because of my enemies.

¹²Do not deliver me to the will of my adversaries; for false witnesses have risen against me, and such as breathe out

will conceal me under the cover of his tent; he will lift me high upon a rock.

⁶And now my head shall be lifted up above my enemies all around me, and I will offer in his tent sacrifices with shouts of joy; I will sing and make melody to the LORD.

⁷Hear, O LORD, when I cry aloud; be gracious to me and answer me!

⁸You have said, "Seek my face." My heart says to you, "Your face, LORD, do I seek."

⁹Hide not your face from me. Turn not your servant away in anger, O you who have been my help. Cast me not off; forsake me not, O God of my salvation!

¹⁰For my father and my mother have forsaken me, but the LORD will take me in.

¹¹Teach me your way, O LORD, and lead me on a level path because of my enemies.

¹²Give me not up to the will of my adversaries; for false witnesses have risen against me,

violence.

and they breathe out violence.

[13]I would have lost heart, unless I had believed that I would see the goodness of the LORD in the land of the living.

[13]I believe that I shall look upon the goodness of the LORD in the land of the living!

[14]Wait on the LORD; be of good courage, and He shall strengthen your heart; wait, I say, on the LORD! *NKJV*

[14]Wait for the LORD; be strong, and let your heart take courage; wait for the LORD! *ESV*

Date _____ Parent/Teacher _____

Shorter Catechism

70. *Q. Which is the seventh commandment?*
    A. The seventh commandment is, "You shall not commit adultery."

71. *Q. What is required in the seventh commandment?*
    A. The seventh commandment requires the preservation of our own and our neighbor's chastity, in heart, speech and behavior.

72. *Q. What is forbidden in the seventh commandment?*
    A. The seventh commandment forbids all unchaste thoughts, words and actions.

73. *Q. Which is the eighth commandment?*
    A. The eighth commandment is, "You shall not steal."

74. *Q. What is required in the eighth commandment?*
    A. The eighth commandment requires the lawful procuring and furthering the wealth and outward estate of ourselves and others.

75. Q. *What is forbidden in the eighth commandment?*
    A. The eighth commandment forbids whatsoever does or may unjustly hinder our own or our neighbor's wealth or outward estate.

76. Q. *Which is the ninth commandment?*
    A. The ninth commandment is, "You shall not give false testimony against your neighbor."

77. Q. *What is required in the ninth commandment?*
    A. The ninth commandment requires the maintaining and promoting of truth between man and man, and of our own and our neighbor's good name, especially in witness bearing.

78. Q. *What is forbidden in the ninth commandment?*
    A. The ninth commandment forbids whatsoever is prejudicial to truth or injurious to our own or our neighbor's good name.

79. Q. *Which is the tenth commandment?*
    A. The tenth commandment is, "You shall not covet your neighbor's house. You shall not covet your neighbor's wife, or his manservant or maidservant, his ox or donkey, or anything that belongs to your neighbor."

80. Q. *What is required in the tenth commandment?*
    A. The tenth commandment requires full contentment with our own condition, with a right and charitable form of spirit toward our neighbor and all that is his.

81. Q. *What is forbidden in the tenth commandment?*
    A. The tenth commandment forbids all discontentment with our own estate, envying or grieving at the good of our neighbor, and all inordinate motions and affections to anything that is his.

82. Q. *Is any man able perfectly to keep the commandments of God?*
    A. No mere man, since the fall, is able in this life perfectly to keep the commandments of God, but does daily break them in thought, word and deed.

83. Q. *Are all transgressions of the law equally heinous?*
    A. Some sins in themselves, and by reason of several aggravations, are more heinous in the sight of God than others.

84. Q. *What does every sin deserve?*
    A. Every sin deserves God's wrath and curse, both in this life and that which is to come.

85. Q. *What does God require of us, that we may escape his wrath and curse, due to us for sin?*
    A. To escape the wrath and curse of God, due to us for sin, God requires of us faith in Jesus Christ, repentance unto life, with the diligent use of all the outward means whereby Christ communicates to us the benefits of redemption.

86. Q. *What is faith in Jesus Christ?*
    A. Faith in Jesus Christ is a saving grace, whereby we receive and rest upon him alone for salvation, as he is offered to us in the gospel.

87. Q. *What is repentance unto life?*
    A. Repentance unto life is a saving grace, whereby a sinner out of a true sense of his sin and apprehension of the mercy of God in Christ, does, with grief and hatred of his sin, turn from it unto God, with full purpose of, and endeavor after, new obedience.

88. Q. *What are the outward and ordinary means whereby Christ communicates to us the benefits of redemption?*

A. The outward and ordinary means whereby Christ communicates to us the benefits of redemption are his ordinances, especially the Word, sacraments and prayer, all which are made effectual to the elect for salvation.

89. *Q. How is the Word made effectual to salvation?*
    A. The Spirit of God makes the reading, but especially the preaching, of the Word, an effectual means of convincing and converting sinners, and of building them up in holiness and comfort, through faith, unto salvation.

90. *Q. How is the Word to be read and heard, that it may become effectual to salvation?*
    A. That the Word may become effectual to salvation, we must attend thereunto with diligence, preparation and prayer; receive it with faith and love; lay it up in our hearts; and practice it in our lives.

Date _____ Parent/Teacher _____

Hymns

"When I Survey the Wondrous Cross"

Date _____ Parent/Teacher _____

"Savior, like a Shepherd Lead Us"

Date _____ Parent/Teacher _____

"Fairest Lord Jesus"

Date _____ Parent/Teacher _____

Grade 7

"Silent Night! Holy Night!"

Date _____ Parent/Teacher _____

"I Belong to Jesus"

Date _____ Parent/Teacher _____

"Holy Bible, Book Divine"

Date _____ Parent/Teacher _____

Supplemental Notes

MEMORY WORK

Grade 8

Read the Gospels of Mark and Luke

Date _____ Parent/Teacher _____

Philippians 2:5–13

⁵Let this mind be in you which was also in Christ Jesus,

⁶who, being in the form of God, did not consider it robbery to be equal with God,

⁷but made Himself of no reputation, taking the form of a servant, and coming in the likeness of men.

⁸And being found in appearance as a man, He humbled Himself and became obedient to the point of death, even the death of the cross.

⁹Therefore God also has highly exalted Him and given Him the name which is above every name,

¹⁰That at the name of Jesus every knee should bow, of those in heaven, and of those

⁵Have this mind among yourselves, which is yours in Christ Jesus,

⁶who, though he was in the form of God, did not count equality with God a thing to be grasped,

⁷but made himself nothing, taking the form of a servant, being born in the likeness of men.

⁸And being found in human form, he humbled himself by becoming obedient to the point of death, even death on a cross.

⁹Therefore God has highly exalted him and bestowed on him the name that is above every name,

¹⁰so that at the name of Jesus every knee should bow, in

on earth, and of those under the earth,

[11]And that every tongue should confess that Jesus Christ is Lord, to the glory of God the Father.

[12]Therefore, my beloved, as you have always obeyed, not as in my presence only, but now much more in my absence, work out your own salvation with fear and trembling;

[13]for it is God who works in you both to will and to do for His good pleasure. *NKJV*

heaven and on earth and under the earth,

[11]and every tongue confess that Jesus Christ is Lord, to the glory of God the Father.

[12]Therefore, my beloved, as you have always obeyed, so now, not only as in my presence but much more in my absence, work out your own salvation with fear and trembling,

[13]for it is God who works in you, both to will and to work for his good pleasure. *ESV*

Date _____ Parent/Teacher _____

Galatians 2:16

Knowing that a man is not justified by the works of the law but by faith in Jesus Christ, even we have believed in Christ Jesus, that we might be justified by faith in Christ and not by the works of the law; for by the works of the law no flesh shall be justified. *NKJV*

Yet we know that a person is not justified by works of the law but through faith in Jesus Christ, so we also have believed in Christ Jesus, in order to be justified by faith in Christ and not by works of the law, because by works of the law no one will be justified. *ESV*

Date _____ Parent/Teacher _____

Ephesians 2:8–10

[8]For by grace you have been saved through faith, and that not of yourselves; it is the gift of God,

[9]not of works, lest anyone should boast.

[10]For we are His workmanship, created in Christ Jesus for good works, which God prepared beforehand that we should walk in them. *NKJV*

[8]For by grace you have been saved through faith. And this is not your own doing; it is the gift of God,

[9]not a result of works, so that no one may boast.

[10]For we are his workmanship, created in Christ Jesus for good works, which God prepared beforehand, that we should walk in them. *ESV*

Date _____ Parent/Teacher _____

2 Corinthians 12:9

And He said to me, "My grace is sufficient for you, for My strength is made perfect in weakness." Therefore most gladly I will rather boast in my infirmities, that the power of Christ may rest upon me. *NKJV*

But he said to me, "My grace is sufficient for you, for my power is made perfect in weakness." Therefore I will boast all the more gladly of my weaknesses, so that the power of Christ may rest upon me. *ESV*

Date _____ Parent/Teacher _____

Isaiah 26: 3, 4

[3]You will keep him in perfect peace, whose mind is stayed

[3]You keep him in perfect peace whose mind is stayed on you,

on You, because he trusts in You.

⁴Trust in the Lᴏʀᴅ forever, for in YAH, the Lᴏʀᴅ, is everlasting strength. *NKJV*

because he trusts in you.

⁴Trust in the Lᴏʀᴅ forever, for the Lᴏʀᴅ Gᴏᴅ is an everlasting rock. *ESV*

Date _____ Parent/Teacher _____

Isaiah 55:6–11

⁶Seek the Lᴏʀᴅ while He may be found, call upon Him while He is near.

⁷Let the wicked forsake his way, and the unrighteous man his thoughts; let him return to the Lᴏʀᴅ, and He will have mercy on him; and to our God, for He will abundantly pardon.

⁸"For My thoughts are not your thoughts, nor are your ways My ways," says the Lᴏʀᴅ.

⁹"For as the heavens are higher than the earth, so are My ways higher than your ways, and My thoughts than your thoughts.

¹⁰For as the rain comes down, and the snow from heaven, and do not return there, but

⁶"Seek the Lᴏʀᴅ while he may be found; call upon him while he is near;

⁷let the wicked forsake his way, and the unrighteous man his thoughts; let him return to the Lᴏʀᴅ, that he may have compassion on him, and to our God, for he will abundantly pardon.

⁸For my thoughts are not your thoughts, neither are your ways my ways, declares the Lᴏʀᴅ.

⁹For as the heavens are higher than the earth, so are my ways higher than your ways and my thoughts than your thoughts.

¹⁰"For as the rain and the snow come down from heaven and

water the earth, and make it bring forth and bud, that it may give seed to the sower and bread to the eater,

[11]so shall My word be that goes forth from My mouth; It shall not return to Me void, but it shall accomplish what I please, and it shall prosper in the thing for which I sent it." *NKJV*

do not return there but water the earth, making it bring forth and sprout, giving seed to the sower and bread to the eater,

[11]so shall my word be that goes out from my mouth; it shall not return to me empty, but it shall accomplish that which I purpose, and shall succeed in the thing for which I sent it." *ESV*

Date _____ Parent/Teacher _____

Shorter Catechism

91. *Q. How do the sacraments become effectual means of salvation?*
    A. The sacraments become effectual means of salvation not from any virtue in them or in him that does administer them, but only by the blessing of Christ and the working of his Spirit in them that by faith receive them.

92. *Q. What is a sacrament?*
    A. A sacrament is a holy ordinance instituted by Christ, wherein by sensible signs Christ and the benefits of the new covenant are represented, sealed and applied to believers.

93. *Q. Which are the sacraments of the New Testament?*
    A. The sacraments of the New Testament are baptism and the Lord's Supper.

94. *Q. What is baptism?*
    A. Baptism is a sacrament, wherein the washing with water in the name of the Father, and of the Son and of

the Holy Spirit does signify and seal our ingrafting into Christ, and partaking of the benefits of the covenant of grace, and our engagement to be the Lord's.

95. Q. *To whom is baptism to be administered?*
   A. Baptism is not to be administered to any that are out of the visible church, till they profess their faith in Christ and obedience to him; but the infants of such as are members of the visible church are to be baptized.

96. Q. *What is the Lord's Supper?*
   A. The Lord's Supper is a sacrament, wherein, by giving and receiving bread and wine according to Christ's appointment, his death is showed forth; and the worthy receivers are—not after a corporal and carnal manner, but by faith—made partakers of his body and blood with all his benefits, to their spiritual nourishment and growth in grace.

97. Q. *What is required to the worthy receiving of the Lord's Supper?*
   A. It is required of them that would worthily partake of the Lord's Supper, that they examine themselves of their knowledge to discern the Lord's body, of their faith to feed upon him, of their repentance, love and new obedience; lest coming unworthily, they eat and drink judgment to themselves.

98. Q. *What is prayer?*
   A. Prayer is the offering up of our desires unto God, for things agreeable to his will, in the name of Christ, with confession of our sins and thankful acknowledgment of his mercies.

99. Q. *What rule has God given for our direction in prayer?*
   A. The whole Word of God is of use to direct us in prayer;

but the special rule of direction is that form of prayer which Christ taught his disciples, commonly called the Lord's Prayer.

100. Q. *What does the preface of the Lord's Prayer teach us?*
 A. The preface of the Lord's Prayer, which is, "Our Father which art in heaven," teaches us to draw near to God with all holy reverence and confidence, as children to a father, able and ready to help us; and that we should pray with and for others.

101. Q. *What do we pray for in the first petition?*
 A. In the first petition, which is, "Hallowed be thy name," we pray that God would enable us and others to glorify him in all that whereby he makes himself known, and that he would dispose of all things to his own glory.

102. Q. *What do we pray for in the second petition?*
 A. In the second petition, which is, "Thy kingdom come," we pray that Satan's kingdom may be destroyed; and that the kingdom of grace may be advanced, ourselves and others brought into it, and kept in it; and that the kingdom of glory may be hastened.

103. Q. *What do we pray for in the third petition?*
 A. In the third petition, which is, "Thy will be done on earth as it is in heaven," we pray that God, by his grace, would make us able and willing to know, obey and submit to his will in all things as the angels do in heaven.

104. Q. *What do we pray for in the fourth petition?*
 A. In the fourth petition, which is, "Give us this day our daily bread," we pray that of God's free gift we may receive a competent portion of the good things of this life and enjoy his blessing with them.

105. Q. *What do we pray for in the fifth petition?*
   A. In the fifth petition, which is, "And forgive us our debts, as we forgive our debtors," we pray that God, for Christ's sake, would freely pardon all our sins; which we are the rather encouraged to ask, because by his grace we are enabled from the heart to forgive others.

106. Q. *What do we pray for in the sixth petition?*
   A. In the sixth petition, which is, "And lead us not into temptation, but deliver us from evil," we pray that God would either keep us from being tempted to sin, or support and deliver us when we are tempted.

107. Q. *What does the conclusion of the Lord's Prayer teach us?*
   A. The conclusion of the Lord's Prayer, which is, "For thine is the kingdom, and the power, and the glory for ever. Amen," teaches us to take our encouragement in prayer from God only, and in our prayers to praise him, ascribing kingdom, power and glory to him; and, in testimony of our desire and assurance to be heard, we say, "Amen."

Date _____ Parent/Teacher _____

Hymns

"Holy, Holy, Holy!"

Date _____ Parent/Teacher _____

"Joy to the World!"

Date _____ Parent/Teacher _____

"The Lord's My Shepherd"

Date _____ Parent/Teacher _____

"I Greet Thee, Who My Sure Redeemer Art"

Date _____ Parent/Teacher _____

Supplemental Notes

MEMORY WORK

Grade 9

Read the Gospel of John and the Acts of the Apostles

Date _____ Parent/Teacher _____

Review the Shorter Catechism, Questions 1–69

Date _____ Parent/Teacher _____

Psalm 46

[1]God is our refuge and strength, a very present help in trouble.

[2]Therefore we will not fear, even though the earth be removed, and though the mountains be carried into the midst of the sea;

[3]though its waters roar and be troubled, though the mountains shake with its swelling.

[4]There is a river whose streams shall make glad the city of God, the holy place of the tabernacle of the Most High.

[5]God is in the midst of her, she shall not be moved; God shall

[1]God is our refuge and strength, a very present help in trouble.

[2]Therefore we will not fear though the earth gives way, though the mountains be moved into the heart of the sea,

[3]though its waters roar and foam, though the mountains tremble at its swelling.

[4]There is a river whose streams make glad the city of God, the holy habitation of the Most High.

[5]God is in the midst of her; she shall not be moved; God will

help her, just at the break of dawn.

⁶The nations raged, the kingdoms were moved; He uttered His voice, the earth melted.

⁷The Lᴏʀᴅ of hosts is with us; the God of Jacob is our refuge.

⁸Come, behold the works of the Lᴏʀᴅ, who has made desolations in the earth.

⁹He makes wars cease to the end of the earth; He breaks the bow and cuts the spear in two; He burns the chariot in the fire.

¹⁰Be still, and know that I am God; I will be exalted among the nations, I will be exalted in the earth!

¹¹The Lᴏʀᴅ of hosts is with us; The God of Jacob is our refuge. *NKJV*

help her when morning dawns.

⁶The nations rage, the kingdoms totter; he utters his voice, the earth melts.

⁷The Lᴏʀᴅ of hosts is with us; the God of Jacob is our fortress.

⁸Come, behold the works of the Lᴏʀᴅ, how he has brought desolations on the earth.

⁹He makes wars cease to the end of the earth; he breaks the bow and shatters the spear; he burns the chariots with fire.

¹⁰"Be still, and know that I am God. I will be exalted among the nations, I will be exalted in the earth!"

¹¹The Lᴏʀᴅ of hosts is with us; the God of Jacob is our fortress. *ESV*

Date _____ Parent/Teacher _____

Galatians 2:20

I have been crucified with Christ; it is no longer I who

I have been crucified with Christ. It is no longer I who

live, but Christ lives in me; and the life which I now live in the flesh I live by faith in the Son of God, who loved me and gave Himself for me. *NKJV*

live, but Christ who lives in me. And the life I now live in the flesh I live by faith in the Son of God, who loved me and gave himself for me. *ESV*

Date _____ Parent/Teacher _____

John 3: 5, 6

[5]Jesus answered, "Most assuredly, I say to you, unless one is born of water and the Spirit, he cannot enter the kingdom of God.

[6]That which is born of the flesh is flesh, and that which is born of the Spirit is spirit." *NKJV*

[5]Jesus answered, "Truly, truly, I say to you, unless one is born of water and the Spirit, he cannot enter the kingdom of God.

[6]That which is born of the flesh is flesh, and that which is born of the Spirit is spirit." *ESV*

Date _____ Parent/Teacher _____

Hymns

"O Come, All Ye Faithful"

Date _____ Parent/Teacher _____

"O for a Thousand Tongues"

Date _____ Parent/Teacher _____

"Jesus Is All the World to Me"

Date _____ Parent/Teacher _____

"To God Be the Glory"

Date _____ Parent/Teacher _____

Supplemental Notes

MEMORY WORK

Grade 10

Read Romans, 1 and 2 Corinthians, Galatians, Ephesians, Philippians, Colossians, and 1 and 2 Thessalonians

Date _____ Parent/Teacher _____

Review the Shorter Catechism, Questions 70–107

Date _____ Parent/Teacher _____

Colossians 1:12–17

[12]Give thanks to the Father who has qualified us to be partakers of the inheritance of the saints in the light.

[13]He has delivered us from the power of darkness and translated us into the kingdom of the Son of His love,

[14]in whom we have redemption through His blood, the forgiveness of sins.

[15]He is the image of the invisible God, the firstborn over all creation.

[16]For by Him all things were created that are in heaven and

[12]Giving thanks to the Father, who has qualified you to share in the inheritance of the saints in light.

[13]He has delivered us from the domain of darkness and transferred us to the kingdom of his beloved Son,

[14]in whom we have redemption, the forgiveness of sins.

[15]He is the image of the invisible God, the firstborn of all creation.

[16]For by him all things were created, in heaven and on earth, visible and invisible,

that are on earth, visible and invisible, whether thrones or dominions or principalities or powers. All things were created through Him and for Him.

[17]And He is before all things, and in Him all things consist. *NKJV*

whether thrones or dominions or rulers or authorities—all things were created through him and for him.

[17]And he is before all things, and in him all things hold together. *ESV*

Date _____ Parent/Teacher _____

Hebrews 12:1, 2

[1]Therefore we also, since we are surrounded by so great a cloud of witnesses, let us lay aside every weight, and the sin which so easily ensnares us, and let us run with endurance the race that is set before us,

[2]looking unto Jesus, the author and finisher of our faith, who for the joy that was set before Him endured the cross, despising the shame, and has sat down at the right hand of the throne of God. *NKJV*

[1]Therefore, since we are surrounded by so great a cloud of witnesses, let us also lay aside every weight, and sin which clings so closely, and let us run with endurance the race that is set before us,

[2]looking to Jesus, the founder and perfecter of our faith, who for the joy that was set before him endured the cross, despising the shame, and is seated at the right hand of the throne of God. *ESV*

Date _____ Parent/Teacher _____

Ecclesiastes 12:1

Remember now your Creator

Remember also your Creator

in the days of your youth, before the difficult days come, and the years draw near when you say, "I have no pleasure in them." *NKJV*

in the days of your youth, before the evil days come and the years draw near of which you will say, "I have no pleasure in them." *ESV*

Date _____ Parent/Teacher _____

1 Corinthians 10:31

Therefore, whether you eat or drink, or whatever you do, do all to the glory of God. *NKJV*

So, whether you eat or drink, or whatever you do, do all to the glory of God. *ESV*

Date _____ Parent/Teacher _____

Joshua 1:9

Have I not commanded you? Be strong and of good courage; do not be afraid, nor be dismayed, for the LORD your God is with you wherever you go. *NKJV*

Have I not commanded you? Be strong and courageous. Do not be frightened, and do not be dismayed, for the LORD your God is with you wherever you go. *ESV*

Date _____ Parent/Teacher _____

Isaiah 57:20, 21

[20]But the wicked are like the troubled sea, when it cannot rest, whose waters cast up mire and dirt.

[20]But the wicked are like the tossing sea; for it cannot be quiet, and its waters toss up mire and dirt.

[21]"There is no peace," says my God, "for the wicked." *NKJV*

[21]"There is no peace," says my God, "for the wicked." *ESV*

Date _____ Parent/Teacher _____

Hymns

"O Come, O Come, Emmanuel"

Date _____ Parent/Teacher _____

"How Great Thou Art"

Date _____ Parent/Teacher _____

"Rock of Ages"

Date _____ Parent/Teacher _____

"A Mighty Fortress"

Date _____ Parent/Teacher _____

Supplemental Notes

MEMORY WORK

Grade 11

Read 1 and 2 Timothy, Titus, Philemon, Hebrews, James, and 1 and 2 Peter

Date _____ Parent/Teacher _____

Review the Shorter Catechism

Date _____ Parent/Teacher _____

Proverbs 3:1–13

¹My son, do not forget my law, but let your heart keep my commands;

²for length of days and long life and peace they will add to you.

³Let not mercy and truth forsake you; bind them around your neck, write them on the tablet of your heart,

⁴And so find favor and high esteem in the sight of God and man.

⁵Trust in the LORD with all your heart, and lean not on your own understanding;

¹My son, do not forget my teaching, but let your heart keep my commandments,

²for length of days and years of life and peace they will add to you.

³Let not steadfast love and faithfulness forsake you; bind them around your neck; write them on the tablet of your heart.

⁴So you will find favor and good success in the sight of God and man.

⁵Trust in the LORD with all your heart, and do not lean on your own understanding.

⁶in all your ways acknowledge Him, and He shall direct your paths.

⁷Do not be wise in your own eyes; fear the L<small>ORD</small> and depart from evil.

⁸It will be health to your flesh, and strength to your bones.

⁹Honor the L<small>ORD</small> with your possessions, and with the firstfruits of all your increase;

¹⁰so your barns will be filled with plenty, and your vats will overflow with new wine.

¹¹My son, do not despise the chastening of the L<small>ORD</small> nor detest His correction;

¹²for whom the L<small>ORD</small> loves He corrects, just as a father the son in whom he delights.

¹³Happy is the man who finds wisdom, and the man who gains understanding. *NKJV*

⁶In all your ways acknowledge him, and he will make straight your paths.

⁷Be not wise in your own eyes; fear the L<small>ORD</small>, and turn away from evil.

⁸It will be healing to your flesh and refreshment to your bones.

⁹Honor the L<small>ORD</small> with your wealth and with the firstfruits of all your produce;

¹⁰then your barns will be filled with plenty, and your vats will be bursting with wine.

¹¹My son, do not despise the L<small>ORD</small>'s discipline or be weary of his reproof,

¹²for the L<small>ORD</small> reproves him whom he loves, as a father the son in whom he delights.

¹³Blessed is the one who finds wisdom, and the one who gets understanding. *ESV*

Date _____ Parent/Teacher _____

Romans 1:16, 17

¹⁶For I am not ashamed of the

¹⁶For I am not ashamed of the

gospel of Christ, for it is the power of God to salvation for everyone who believes, for the Jew first and also for the Greek.

[17]For in it the righteousness of God is revealed from faith to faith; as it is written, "The just shall live by faith." *NKJV*

gospel, for it is the power of God for salvation to everyone who believes, to the Jew first and also to the Greek.

[17]For in it the righteousness of God is revealed from faith for faith, as it is written, "The righteous shall live by faith." *ESV*

Date _____ Parent/Teacher _____

Galatians 5:14

For all the law is fulfilled in one word, even in this: "You shall love your neighbor as yourself." *NKJV*

For the whole law is fulfilled in one word: "You shall love your neighbor as yourself." *ESV*

Date _____ Parent/Teacher _____

Hymns

"Praise Him! Praise Him!"

Date _____ Parent/Teacher _____

"O Sacred Head, Now Wounded"

Date _____ Parent/Teacher _____

"Blest Be the Tie That Binds"

Date _____ Parent/Teacher _____

"Wonderful Grace of Jesus"

Date _____ Parent/Teacher _____

Supplemental Notes

MEMORY WORK

Grade 12

Read 1, 2 and 3 John, Jude and Revelation

Date _____ Parent/Teacher _____

Review the Shorter Catechism

Date _____ Parent/Teacher _____

Romans 10:9–11

[9]If you confess with your mouth the Lord Jesus and believe in your heart that God has raised Him from the dead, you will be saved.

[10]For with the heart one believes to righteousness, and with the mouth confession is made to salvation.

[11]For the Scripture says, "Whoever believes on Him will not be put to shame." *NKJV*

[9]If you confess with your mouth that Jesus is Lord and believe in your heart that God raised him from the dead, you will be saved.

[10]For with the heart one believes and is justified, and with the mouth one confesses and is saved.

[11]For the Scripture says, "Everyone who believes in him will not be put to shame." *ESV*

Date _____ Parent/Teacher _____

Matthew 25:31–40

31When the Son of Man comes in His glory, and all the holy angels with Him, then He will sit on the throne of His glory.

32All the nations will be gathered before Him, and He will separate them one from another, as a shepherd divides his sheep from the goats.

33And He will set the sheep on His right hand, but the goats on the left.

34Then the King will say to those on His right hand, "Come, you blessed of My Father, inherit the kingdom prepared for you from the foundation of the world:

35for I was hungry and you gave Me food; I was thirsty and you gave Me drink; I was a stranger and you took Me in;

36I was naked and you clothed Me; I was sick and you visited Me; I was in prison and you came to Me."

37Then the righteous will answer Him, saying "Lord, when did we see You hungry and

31When the Son of Man comes in his glory, and all the angels with him, then he will sit on his glorious throne.

32Before him will be gathered all the nations, and he will separate people one from another as a shepherd separates the sheep from the goats.

33And he will place the sheep on his right, but the goats on the left.

34Then the King will say to those on his right, "Come, you who are blessed by my Father, inherit the kingdom prepared for you from the foundation of the world.

35For I was hungry and you gave me food, I was thirsty and you gave me drink, I was a stranger and you welcomed me,

36I was naked and you clothed me, I was sick and you visited me, I was in prison and you came to me."

37Then the righteous will answer him, saying, "Lord, when

feed You, or thirsty and give You drink?

38When did we see You a stranger and take You in, or naked and clothe You?

39Or when did we see You sick, or in prison, and come to You?"

40And the King will answer and say to them, "Assuredly, I say to you, inasmuch as you did it to one of the least of these My brethren, you did it to Me." *NKJV*

did we see you hungry and feed you, or thirsty and give you drink?

38And when did we see you a stranger and welcome you, or naked and clothe you?

39And when did we see you sick or in prison and visit you?"

40And the King will answer them, "Truly, I say to you, as you did it to one of the least of these my brothers, you did it to me." *ESV*

Date _____ Parent/Teacher _____

Colossians 3:1–4

1If then you were raised with Christ, seek those things which are above, where Christ is, sitting at the right hand of God.

2Set your mind on things above, not on things on the earth.

3For you died, and your life is hidden with Christ in God.

1If then you have been raised with Christ, seek the things that are above, where Christ is, seated at the right hand of God.

2Set your minds on things that are above, not on things that are on earth.

3For you have died, and your life is hidden with Christ in God.

[4]When Christ who is our life appears, then you also will appear with Him in glory. *NKJV*

[4]When Christ who is your life appears, then you also will appear with him in glory. *ESV*

Date _____ Parent/Teacher _____

Hymns

"O Worship the King"

Date _____ Parent/Teacher _____

"Lord, Thou Hast Been Our Dwelling Place"

Date _____ Parent/Teacher _____

"For All the Saints"

Date _____ Parent/Teacher _____

"God Be Merciful to Me"

Date _____ Parent/Teacher _____

Supplemental Notes

APPENDIX A

List of Memory Work in *Memory Work Notebook*

Listed below is the Scripture and other memory work found in this Notebook, together with its location.